Questions from Your Cosmic Dance

JOHN COLEMAN

HAZELDEN®

Hazelden
Center City, Minnesota 55012-0176

1-800-328-0094

1-612-257-1331
(24-hour FAX)

http://www.hazelden.org
(World Wide Web site on Internet)

Library of Congress Cataloging-in-Publication Data
Coleman, John, 1961–
    Questions from your cosmic dance / John Coleman.
        p.   cm.
    Includes index.
    ISBN: 1-56838-143-3
    1. Conduct of life—Miscellanea.   2. Peace of Mind—
Miscellanea.   I. Title.
BJ1595.C667   1997
291.4'32—dc21   96-39580
                                                                        CIP

02 01 00 99 98 97   9 8 7 6 5 4 3 2 1

Book design by Will H. Powers
Typesetting by Stanton Publication Services, Inc.
Cover design by David Spohn

Editor's Note
Hazelden offers a variety of information on chemical dependency
and related areas. Our publications do not necessarily represent
Hazelden's programs, nor do they officially speak for any Twelve Step
organization.

Questions from Your Cosmic Dance

For Kathy, Elena, and Micah

Acknowledgments

The author gratefully acknowledges publishers of the following authors for permission to quote brief passages from their works:

George Appleton. From *The Oxford Book of Prayer,* edited by George Appleton, © 1985. Reprinted by permission of Oxford University Press.

Eknath Easwaran. From *Gandhi the Man,* © 1972. Reprinted by permission of Nilgiri Press, Tomales, CA 94971.

Brennan R. Hill, Paul Knitter, and William Madges. From *Faith, Religion, & Theology: A Contemporary Introduction,* © 1990. Reprinted by permission of Twenty-Third Publications, P.O. Box 180, Mystic, CT 06355.

Thomas Keating. From *Open Heart, Open Mind,* © 1986 and 1992. Reprinted by permission of The Continuum Publishing Company.

Rigoberta Menchu. From *I, Rigoberta Menchu,* edited by Elisabeth Burgos-Debray, © 1984. Reprinted by permission of the publishers, Verso.

. . . *no despair of ours can alter the reality of things, or stain the joy of the cosmic dance which is always there. Indeed, we are in the midst of it, and it is in the midst of us, for it beats in our very blood, whether we want it to or not.*

Yet the fact remains that we are invited to forget ourselves on purpose, cast our awful solemnity to the winds and join in the general dance.

THOMAS MERTON

Introduction

In the spring of 1988, I should have been happy and content. My wife, Kathy, was pregnant with our first child, we had just contracted to buy our first home, and I had a good job as a college teacher. Even then I knew I should have been looking forward to the future, but I felt miserable. What was worse, as the date of our closing and Kathy's due date approached, I began having anxiety attacks.

Soon I was diagnosed as having an anxiety disorder. Despite having blessings that many people long for, I had lost all peace in my life. I wandered miserably through my days and just tried to hold things together. Within a year or so I had the anxiety more or less under control, but I was still intensely sad. Never mind that I loved my wife and newborn daughter. Never mind that I looked forward to coming home at the end of each day. Never mind that I had a warm, comfortable home in a safe neighborhood. I was bone sad, spirit sad.

Somewhere in the midst of this suffering I decided that the purpose of my life would be to find out how to be at peace. Although I never actually articulated my decision, I knew on an intuitive level that I needed to read, to observe, to listen. "What does it take," I asked myself, "to be at peace in this life? What am I doing wrong? Why am I not at peace?"

I learned several things early on. First, there is no specific recipe for spiritual peace. Contented people tend to share similar qualities or habits, but beyond these every person has to find her or his own path to peace. Second, faith in God (or at least faith in *something*) is necessary. Third, counting on God to change the facts of life so that we can be happy constitutes a false faith that's bound to disappoint. Finally, most of us already have all that we need to be at peace. Since the God of heaven and earth is always with us, then the cosmic dance of peace and joy Merton writes of is going on endlessly around us and within us. The problem is, we get lost on our way to the dance floor.

Over the next few years my search for peace slowly led to many new discoveries. I know that all of the lessons from my journey may not apply to everybody's situation. For that reason, this is a book of questions. I don't want to claim that this book contains a plan for peace. Anyone who tries to sell you "the peace diet" is being misleading, wittingly or unwittingly.

The approach I've used in *Questions from Your Cosmic Dance* is to (1) ask a question, (2) explain why the question is relevant to a person's peace journey and suggest an answer, and (3) offer a quotation that addresses the question in a memorable or interesting fashion.

While reading you may notice that the issues addressed echo one another and overlap considerably. That's as it should be. Finding peace is a disorganized business, and insights gained in one situation often apply to others as well. Important questions, then, are sometimes asked in different ways throughout the book. In fact, a handful of questions are, in my judgment, crucial to spiritual peace, and these we return to in the form of "echo questions."

Since the peace journey includes lots of detours and double backs, don't get worried about marking pages carefully or reading the book from start to finish. You can start in the middle and read to both ends if you like. I've written the questions in a purposeful order, but that was more out of my own sense of obligation to "have a plan" than out of any sound rationale for going step by step.

Asking myself these questions has changed my life. I now have two children: an eight-year-old daughter, Elena, and a five-year-old son, Micah. I still love my wife, Kathy, and live in the same house we bought in 1988. I still teach writing at a small liberal arts college, where I also counsel students about academic success. I find myself asking them many of the questions that I ask you here.

Although the circumstances of my life have not changed substantially since I began this journey, I am happier and more at peace now than I have ever been. I'm trying to spend each moment of each day on the cosmic dance floor, where we can all be light and free in God's presence. I pray that we will see each other there.

Author's Notes

Although I am a college writing teacher, I am a confirmed hater of stuffy, overly formal prose. For this reason, I purposefully ignore a couple of longstanding stylistic conventions of the English language: (1) "Never use 'you' as an indefinite pronoun referring to the reader." Sorry, I use "you" to address the reader. I find it more comfortable and somehow closer to the truth than the more educated and distant "one." (2) "Be consistent in the use of pronouns." Sorry again, but I drift back and forth between the pronouns "we" and "you." When I say "we," I mean "most people searching for peace, myself included." When I say "you," I am addressing the reader personally. If you get nuts when people play fast and loose with the Queen's English, see question 124.

I also want to say a word here about gender-sensitive language. You may notice that many of the people quoted in this book use "man" or "men" to signify "humanity." Most of these individuals were born, lived, and died before issues of gender neutrality in writing and speaking were thought up. Their ideas are profound, their styles dandy, but they just didn't see the pimples on their work that we see today. I'm going to be bold enough to ask you to forgive them and, if necessary, me for including them. As for my position on gender and language, you will discover that shortly.

Questions from Your Cosmic Dance

*Does your body get tense with all the tasks
you try to accomplish each day?*

Often we get so caught up in moments of stress that
we hurry around and tense up even when stressful
times have passed. Every now and then we need to
take note of the tension level in our bodies and make
it a point to breathe deeply and relax. If we fail to do
so, we can spend a whole day feeling miserable just
because of some minor irritation like heavy traffic on
the way to work.

◎◎

Make haste slowly.
SUETONIUS

2

Do you know your own body?

Though the Christian tradition during various periods has espoused mortification of the flesh, the body is actually one of our best mental and spiritual directors. If we pay attention, our bodies let us know when we're troubled or anxious. We get headaches, backaches, nausea, fatigue. The temptation is to ignore or medicate such ills, yet heeding their message can lead to greater self-knowledge.

For example, let's say that every time you go out to lunch with a close friend you come home wiped out. Unless you eat way too much when you dine out, chances are your body is trying to tell you something about what's going on in the back of your mind. Maybe your friend is a real talker and you spend all of your time with her or him struggling to pay attention. This simple observation as well as dozens of others you can make by just knowing your body is educational and peace giving.

@@

If "mind" acts on body, then all physical laws are invalid.
JOHN BROADUS WATSON

*If you sit still for more than a few moments,
do you feel the need to get up and do something?*

Many people want inner peace, yet feel uncomfortable sitting still long enough to really rest. If you get fidgety easily, you need to practice resting and relaxing. After all, you can't expect to find spiritual peace until you learn to quiet your body.

◎◎

You do not need to leave your room. Remain sitting at your table and listen. Do not even listen, simply wait. Do not even wait, be quite still and solitary. The world will freely offer itself to you to be unmasked, it has no choice, it will roll in ecstasy at your feet.

FRANZ KAFKA

How much can you accomplish by sitting still?

I have a friend who works down the hall from me, and sometimes when she pokes her head in my office, she sees me leaning back in my desk chair with my eyes closed. She always says the same thing: "Preparing for class again, huh, John?" Actually, I am.

Over the past few years I've found that I can get tons of work done by relaxing, closing my eyes, breathing deeply, and letting my mind work on a task. I make an effort to avoid sitting hunched over my desk and staring with furrowed brow at papers or a computer screen. Instead I do my thinking first and then immediately take notes on what I've come up with. In this way I'm often able to work and rest at the same time.

I realize that this technique isn't possible with every job, but for mind work at least, the body needn't be clenched and strained.

◎◎

Wisdom's self oft seeks to sweet retired solitude. . . .
JOHN MILTON

*Is the radio always on in the car
and the television always on at home?*

Noise is a reliable companion, but eventually you have to be quiet and listen to what your body and soul want to tell you. What you learn in moments of silence can be painful or disturbing. You might realize that you are lonely, dissatisfied with your job, or disappointed with a relationship. Painful memories you thought were all behind you sometimes resurface. On the flip side, peace and contentment are also frequent visitors to silence. Whatever you experience in quiet moments, you can't run from reality or from yourself.

@@

*He is nearest to the gods
who knows how to be silent.*
MARCUS PORCIUS CATO

*Do you ever listen to silence
and its accompaniment?*

Every day the sounds of children laughing, wind swirling, and our own hearts beating go unappreciated. Such sounds, the accompaniment of silence, are food for a soul that's hungry for peace. When we close our mouths, we open our ears to the voice of God, who says "love" and "joy" to us in more ways than we can imagine.

❀

*I have calmed and quieted my soul,
like a child quieted at its mother's breast:
like a child that is quieted is my soul.*

PSALM 131:2

What does your voice sound like?

Nearly every day we hear conversations in the distance. Sometimes we can't hear the words being said, but we can guess the intensity of the discussion by the sounds of the voices. We can tell if people are angry, carefree, rushed, or secretive just by noting volume and pitch.

When people hear your voice through walls, what do they hear? Of course, we all have grouchy days, but people overhearing us should generally sense our peace journey. Listen to your own voice. Not everybody should sound like Fred Rogers, but everyone who seeks peace should use the voice as an instrument to give peace to others, not to pollute the air with hostility and impatience.

☙❧

Speech is a mirror of the soul:
as a man speaks, so is he.
PUBLILIUS SYRUS

Is silence your teacher?

A monkey sticks its hand through a hole in a box. It searches for a moment and grabs an apple. Eager to eat, it tries to pull the apple from the box, but it won't fit. The monkey fixates on the apple and repeatedly jerks its hand, trying to squeeze it and the apple through the hole. After a long time, the monkey catches on: *let go* of the apple, and the hand will fit back through the hole—freedom.

Our minds work this way too. We see something we want (e.g., a possession, a solution), we grab hold, and we skin our lives trying to jerk it out of the box. Only in letting go can we *begin* to retrieve what's in the box; in fact, when we let go, stand back, and look at the box, we might find what we need overflowing, running down the side.

Only silence of mind and body can teach us this. Only when we stop and listen can we climb out of our own paradigm of self-interest and fear and into God's paradigm of the unexpected, of light and life, of courage and compassion.

ൟ

The human heart has hidden treasures,
In secret kept, in silence sealed.
CHARLOTTE BRONTË

*Are you a good judge
of when to speak
and when to remain silent?*

Some of the noise that clutters our environment comes from sirens, machinery, cars, and stereos, but much of it comes from ourselves. Although we're often tempted to blame "this crazy world" for noise pollution, we need to remember that some of the most damaging sounds come from our own mouths. When our words unnecessarily hurt others, we are worse than the neighbor's dog who barks at 3 A.M. and disrupts our night's sleep. The dog doesn't know any better. When we insult or ridicule, we are the worst noise pollution of all, for we cause immediate and purposeful harm.

෨෨

*He knows not how to speak who cannot be silent. . . .
Loudness is impotence.*
JOHANN KASPAR LAVATER

Can you let a good point remain unspoken?

When we have an idea to contribute to a discussion, it burns in our throats until we can let it out. Often our idea will really develop the conversation and be of use to those who hear it. Other times, however, we want to throw in our two cents simply for the sake of vanity. I suspect this is why business meetings have such a notorious reputation. People get together and at once lose sight of their goal—to accomplish something. Instead, they see who can sound the smartest.

When I get an idea or remark that's trying to force its way through my lips, I try to ask myself the following question: "Am I really trying to contribute, or am I trying to look good?"

@@

I have learned silence from the talkative, toleration from the intolerant, and kindness from the unkind; yet strange, I am ungrateful to those teachers.
KAHLIL GIBRAN

When somebody is talking,
are you really listening?

The next time you have a conversation, observe whether you are really listening. Here's how you can tell: if you're always thinking about what you're going to say next, then you're listening more to yourself than to the other person. Try to lose yourself in what others are saying.

◎◎

Avoid interruptive thinking. Everyone—and I mean everyone—has something good to offer you if you are astute enough to find it. Sometimes it means picking a small kernel out of a lot of chaff, but the kernel is always there. One way to get the best from people is to learn to avoid what I call interruptive thinking. This is where someone is saying something to you and you interrupt—and probably change the subject in doing so.

DAVID MAHONEY

Are you a nonthreatening listener?

I believe that we as human beings feel a need to connect with one another. We want others to share in our experiences—good and bad. For this reason we tell each other our joys and sorrows, not primarily because we want somebody else to manage our lives for us, but because we long for the unconditional presence of another in our world. We don't want to feel alone.

Yet often we rob each other of this communion because we feel somehow obligated to judge what others tell us. After all, we figure, if my friend is letting me know about a problem, he or she must want me to help solve it. In my experience, people don't generally want such intrusion; they want generosity of heart.

If we have advice to offer, we can always say, "I've got an idea. Want to hear it?" Lots of times, in fact, people will say, "Sure, what do you think?" But when we force our ideas on others, our words can rob ourselves and those we love of the opportunity to connect.

@@

Beware lest clamour be taken for counsel.
DESIDERIUS ERASMUS

*Do you get caught up in the world's frantic pace
and believe that you're not getting much
accomplished unless you're rushing around?*

When we applaud the "efficiency" of driving eighty miles per hour or the convenience of ordering, receiving, and eating a hamburger in three minutes, we've fallen into the trap of assuming that fast is best. However, senseless speed does nothing but knot up our bodies and steal our peace. The next time you are in a hurry, notice the tension in your muscles (especially in your neck, arms, and abdomen) and in your mind.

◎◎

*Stillest streams
Oft water the fairest meadows, and the bird
That flutters least is longest on the wing.*
WILLIAM COWPER

14

Have you ever taken notice of nature's pace?

Someday when you get the chance, go to the woods and sit under a tree for about half an hour. Force yourself. Why is it that people measure time in nanoseconds and the rest of creation measures time in millennia? If you'd look around, you'd see saplings, fallen trees, maybe even a chipmunk or deer. Everything is growing, moving at its own pace. Take a deer, for example. A deer isn't constantly checking its watch, eating on the run, or cramming its days with activities. A deer is living in its moment. (Now who's the dumb animal?) When you leave the woods, take a little of its patient, free spirit with you.

❡❡

There is no joy but calm!
ALFRED, LORD TENNYSON

Are you looking at what's in front of you?

Have you ever looked closely at the hands of an elderly person? Years rub the skin, which grows thin and fragile. It almost ripples over the flesh and bone. The knuckles of the arthritic hands blossom. Such hands, perhaps in pain, hold the smooth faces of children. Such hands struggle to hold pens, and we see an odd beauty in the effort of the cramped writing.

Gifts like the hands of the aged, the long eyelashes of children, the whistling of the guy next door, they tumble over one another and land about us. We generally step over them and move on.

@@

God hides things by putting them near us.
RALPH WALDO EMERSON

Can you find fifteen minutes per day to sit quietly and relax?

To join the cosmic dance that Thomas Merton writes about, the dance of lightness and joy, you need to get to know the cosmos and yourself. You need to sit still and clear your mind. You need to listen. Fifteen minutes of peace a day is a minimum, a small serving, a spiritual hors d'oeuvre, but you'd be surprised at the benefits of this quarter of an hour. You learn how your body and mind ought to feel, and develop the ability to bring yourself to a reasonably peaceful state even in times of stress. In other words, if you are faithful to giving yourself pockets of peace during the day, you acquire the habit of bringing peace to all that you do.

◎◎

Be still, and know that I am God.
PSALM 46:10

Who is your God?

If you grew up learning about a bearded, wrathful God, it's pretty hard to move toward spiritual peace. You might see God as holding some sort of heavenly clipboard with all of your sins from birth to death duly noted. When you stop and really think about it, however, it becomes clear that this viewpoint is a trivialization of and insult to God. After all, what sort of God would create you and all the beauty of the universe so that you could trudge around every day with the thought of damnation always hanging over your head? The question for the day, then, is, who do you *really* think God is? Of course, you have to answer this question for yourself, but let me tell you my answer. My God is neither male nor female exclusively. Like all mothers and fathers, my God is a fool, in love with the children, desperate that they should be happy and at peace. Punishment is the last thing on my God's mind. I don't know whether my God is pulling strings and making things happen, and I don't care. Finally, my God is not only with us, but a part of us—I mean physically and spiritually. Three words of Saint Paul, which appear below, define my God.

֍

God is love.
THE FIRST LETTER OF JOHN

Will you claim your divinity?

History has taught us that power is conducive to corruption. For this reason, talk of claiming divinity can raise red flags all over the place. The danger is eliminated, however, when we acknowledge the God in all people and when we realize the cost of this incarnation.

God within doesn't give us our way, but calls us to see God in others. God within doesn't give us authority, but makes us servants. God within doesn't make us judges, but lets us see our own frailties. To claim divinity, then, is to see the waves of healing and redemption splashing over all that is.

◎◎

The presence of God in His world as its Creator depends on no one but Him. His presence in the world as Man depends, in some measure, upon men. Not that we can do anything to change the mystery of the Incarnation in itself: but we are able to decide whether we ourselves, and that portion of the world which is ours, shall become aware of His presence, consecrated by it, and transfigured by its light.

THOMAS MERTON

What kinds of things do you pray for?

Many of us pray for *things*—things to go our way, things to change, things to possess. But let's face it, praying for the fulfillment of our own will is a dead end. People get sick, pray to get better, then die. People suffer emotionally, pray for their pain to cease, and go through pain anyway. Obviously, the way to pray is *not* to pray for our circumstances to change, but for our spirits to change. Rely on God for strength, courage, peace—the things God will provide. Don't make God your request line.

☮☮

For all that has been—Thanks!
For all that shall be—Yes!
DAG HAMMARSKJÖLD

Do you struggle to control matters over which you have no control?

If you examine your life, you'll notice that you have little control over what affects you on a daily basis. When a loved one is disappointed by a failure, for example, your own peace of mind can be sent into tailspin, yet ultimately you probably have no control over the situation. Or consider another example. Let's say you interview for a job and get the feeling that you're really in the running, only to find out that the position was filled from within the company, as had been planned all along. You pray for the job, don't get it, and feel that either you or God is to blame. Unfortunately, such anguish is the inevitable result of praying for your own wishes. Since God doesn't grant your request, you assume that God isn't listening and may not exist at all. As the famous quotation below states, we shouldn't pray for control, but for the qualities that enable us to deal with reality.

@∕9

God, give us grace to accept with serenity the things that cannot be changed, courage to change the things which should be changed, and the wisdom to distinguish the one from the other.
REINHOLD NIEBUHR

What is control?

Nearly every attempt I have seen at control has done more damage than good. The examples are so numerous that, for me, the issue is beyond debate, but here's one case to consider: political strategists talk about "spin control," which is a way of presenting reality to shape public opinion. It's soft selling the truth; it's actually a euphemism for a lie. What's the end result of spin control? Widespread mistrust of politicians and confusion about what they as individuals stand for. Worst of all, some in public office are so concerned with pinching the facts that their only real "stand" becomes re-election. Who really benefits from spin control?

I don't mean to paint all politicians with broad strokes, but to make a point: in both public and personal affairs, control is an illusion. Gain power in one area; create a malignancy in another. "Reality" and "truth," as best we can recognize them, are most often infected or compromised by attempts to control them.

☙☙

Beware lest you lose the substance
by grasping at the shadow.
AESOP

What is power?

Many people live under the impression that the more objects and people they control, the more power they have, but there's a problem with this philosophy. People who are hungry for power never gain as much power as they would like. So who is more powerful, the person who appears to control much and is desperate to control more, or the person who controls little but is content?

⊚⊚

My greatest weapon is mute prayer.
MAHATMA GANDHI

23

What is prayer?

While many of us think of prayer as our way of letting God know what God ought to do for us, others see prayer on the level of a nightcap or milk and cookies before bed—something comfy to do before hitting the sack. If, however, we think of prayer as an attempt to commune with God, then we can be praying all the time. Prayer is an openness to the presence of God, and we can enter into that gentle, healing presence in all that we do; in fact, our actions themselves, even our daily work can be prayer if we direct our hearts toward God. Provided we're not harming others or ourselves, we can always be dancing with God.

@/@

Orare est laborare, laborare est orare.
[To pray is to work, to work is to pray.]
SAINT BENEDICT

*Have you ever felt the need to pray, but
didn't have anything in particular to pray for?*

You don't need words to pray. You don't need a goal to pray. Many people, myself included, find the most meaningful prayer to be one in which you sit quietly and think of as little as possible. This is called "contemplative prayer," and its only goal is to rest in God's presence. No words are necessary. If you go to the library and look for books by Basil Pennington, Thomas Keating, and Thomas Merton (among many others), you can learn about contemplative prayer (also called "centering prayer").

☺☺

The root of prayer is interior silence.
THOMAS KEATING

*Do you torment yourself wondering
why things happen the way they do?*

Many of us tell ourselves that God has a plan for our lives and that things happen for a reason. The truth is, we have no idea why good and bad things happen to us and to others. *Candide,* a literary work by Voltaire, focuses on this very question. After a litany of gruesome, implausible, darkly humorous misadventures, Candide, the work's protagonist, concludes that it's best not to waste time trying to figure out why things happen. Such answers are beyond us. His way of saying that we should just concentrate on matters of the here and now appears below.

@@

We must cultivate our garden.
VOLTAIRE

Do you cling too tightly to small comforts?

Exaggerating the importance of any single detail in our lives is a sign of a spiritual disturbance. For example, people who are very unhappy might spend an inordinate amount of time cleaning the house, washing the car, manicuring the garden, making sure their kids are dressed and groomed perfectly, or tanning their own bodies. Obviously, the list could go on.

All of these concerns in moderation may be noble, but there comes a moment when attention turns to obsession, which is a symptom of an infection of sadness. The person who has a hemorrhage every time a kid dribbles grape juice on her clothes needs to sit still for a good half hour and ask, "Okay, what's really wrong here?"

@@

> *Wandering in a vast forest at night,*
> *I have only a faint light to guide me.*
> *A stranger appears and says to me:*
> *"My friend, you should blow out your candle*
> *in order to find your way more clearly."*
> *This stranger is a theologian.*
> DENIS DIDEROT

*Does your memory of the past sometimes
ruin your experience in the present?*

Each day many of us lug around the weight of our past sorrows and failures. Although this is normal, it often prevents us from realizing our potential. We assume that if we've done something poorly in the past, we will automatically do it poorly in the present. Mathematics is a good example. Studies indicate that college students with difficulties in math almost always report a very painful or embarrassing experience in a math class from grammar or high school. There is good news, though. We don't need to be held captive by the past. If we understand how the past makes us apprehensive in the present, we gradually empower ourselves to leave painful memories behind us and to realize our potential.

@⊘

*Ne'er look for birds of this year
in the nests of the last.*
MIGUEL DE CERVANTES

Does your present often get swallowed up
by worries about the future?

Just as many people drag the past around behind them, so too many shove the future's burden of uncertainty and fear before them. If this is true of you, then the idea of living in what Dr. Norman Vincent Peale calls "day-tight compartments" will change your life. For example, if you find that you must move to another state but aren't sure if you will be happy there, the idea that you may have to stay there forever might be crushing. However, if you say to yourself, "Today I'll live in this new place, but I might be somewhere else tomorrow," then life is a bit lighter. Although conventional wisdom's advice that you plan ahead has some merit, planning ahead often turns into worrying ahead. Think about the future a bit if you must, but don't assume anything about the next year or even the next week. Assume instead that today you must live and love abundantly, and remember, all things in this world are temporary.

✿✿

So do not worry about tomorrow,
for tomorrow will bring worries of its own.
Today's trouble is enough for today.
MATTHEW 6:34

Are you waiting to be happy?

Many of us are afraid of the future, but at the same time we look forward to it, believing that happiness is just around the corner—when our kids are out of diapers, when we get all our debts paid off, when we can afford a BMW, when we fall in love with the right person, or when we retire. The problem is, we can wait our whole lives to be happy and never quite get around to it. We're in such a hurry to get to tomorrow's happiness, we forget to be happy today.

◎◎

What is destructive is impatience, haste,
expecting too much too fast.
MAY SARTON

Is what you're doing
at this very moment important?

As you read this book, you are on a peace journey. You are thinking about your life, exploring your attitudes and beliefs. Your eyes are set on the cosmic dance, which is God's will for us. If you look at what you're doing in this light, then this is one of the most important moments of your life. Spending time on your spiritual health and happiness is like a farmer preparing the soil for planting. If the soil is rich and tilled, crops can grow very well. Same with your life. If your spirit, the soil of your life, is nourished by God and examined by yourself, then acts of kindness and a peaceful, joyful disposition can grow from you.

@⦾

I have no expectation that any man will read history aright who thinks that what was done in a remote age, by men whose names have resounded far, has any deeper sense than what he is doing today.
RALPH WALDO EMERSON

Do you give yourself credit for growing?

Because all of us keep making aggravating mistakes, it's hard to see how we are stronger and wiser today than we were yesterday. It's difficult, for example, to see how our latest unwarranted outburst of anger has made us wise, until we find ourselves forgiving the same fault in a loved one. Such failures enrich us if we don't allow them to dominate the present. Today, think of one way you have grown because of your mistakes in the past year.

৩৶

A man should never be ashamed to own he has been in the wrong, which is but saying, in other words, that he is wiser today than he was yesterday.
ALEXANDER POPE

Are you patient?

The next seven questions concern Saint Paul's definition of love, which is found in the first of his two letters to the Corinthians. Although Saint Paul wrote his letters for a fairly specific purpose, to end conflict among the churches of Corinth, his ideas about love are worth examining individually and applying to our own relationships.

The first quality Paul presents is patience. Where love is concerned, patience is recognizing and letting go of annoyance and anger with other people's failure to live up to our standards or to meet our needs. If you are always bothered by the behavior of others, you are not loving well; moreover, you are imposing unnecessary tension on yourself. Looking at all people through the eyes of love allows you to chuckle at and short-circuit your own silly impatience.

@@

Love is patient.
1 CORINTHIANS 13:4

Are you kind?

Do you try to understand people and see them in the best and most complimentary light? For example, when you see a drug abuser on television, do you blame the abuser or do you wonder about the painful circumstances that brought the person to the point of destruction? Kindness means giving people the benefit of the doubt and being compassionate even when you have a feeling people don't deserve it.

◎◎

Love is kind.
1 CORINTHIANS 13:4

Are you envious or boastful or arrogant or rude?

All of these qualities stem from a single attribute: self-centeredness, a big peace stealer. When we're envious of the beautiful house our friend just bought, we permit another person's good fortune to bother us. Rather than celebrating our friend's happiness, envy makes us wonder why we're not so lucky. Sometimes envy even makes us celebrate our friends' failures. Love means getting out of ourselves and into the joy of others.

◎◎

Love is not envious or boastful or arrogant or rude.
1 CORINTHIANS 13:4–5

Do you often insist on having things your own way?

I suspect that most people don't think the "my way or no way" philosophy is a failure of love, but it is. After all, what are some of the best ways to demonstrate love? To share power, to accommodate, to sacrifice. These acts make us vulnerable because they demand that we give up control over those we claim to love. Nobody likes vulnerability, but without it, love is stunted and unfulfilling.

෨෧

Love does not insist on its own way.
1 CORINTHIANS 13:5

Are you irritable or resentful?

Being irritable or resentful means that you are thinking of yourself before others. For example, if you become irritable when your five-year-old child sings the same song over and over again, your feeling isn't based on anything wrong with the child and what he or she is doing, but on your own needs. Although you can't help but get annoyed at hearing the twenty-third rendition of "Mary Had a Little Lamb," you can see the frustration for what it is and sing along rather than shout.

◎◎

Love is not irritable or resentful.
1 CORINTHIANS 13:5

*Do you seek the truth,
even though it may be painful?*

When people love one another, sometimes they try to cheer each other up. After all, nobody likes to see a loved one in pain; however, when we avoid painful truths and try to protect others from them as well, we risk hurting ourselves and others. Hopefully the truths we encounter in life are positive, but resisting a painful truth only serves to muffle pain which must be experienced. If we wish to act out our love for others selflessly and courageously, we must be willing to enter into their pain with them. If we wish to be loving to ourselves, we must suffer through difficult truths.

@@

*Love does not rejoice in wrongdoing,
but it rejoices in truth.*
1 CORINTHIANS 13:6

Do you love abundantly?

Saint Paul's definition of love holds up pretty well regardless of one's religious orientation. In fact, you may have noticed that the passage from which the last seven quotations are taken is often read at weddings of people from many Christian denominations. The final quotation from that passage, which appears below, demonstrates the bottomless nature of love. There's no great challenge in loving others during times of joy and prosperity, but what about during periods of conflict? According to Paul, love continues regardless of the immediate circumstances. One qualification is in order, however. Love does not require that we remain in abusive or destructive relationships. When we're being abused or destroyed, then for the sake of ourselves *and* our loved one, we may need to let love lead us from the relationship.

※

Love bears all things, believes all things,
hopes all things, endures all things.
1 CORINTHIANS 13:7

Who and what are you in love with?

It is a staggering understatement to remark that unful-filling relationships can be a major obstacle to spiritual peace. We find ourselves at times stumbling through our days, wondering how our romantic and platonic loves can leave us feeling desolate. "If I'm supposed to be in love," we think, "why do I feel so alone?"

I don't have a solution to this human dilemma, but I have an answer to the question. In a relationship we long for connection, communion with another, but sometimes all we commune with is our own need for security, consideration, and approval. It's hard to meet these needs in isolation, so we find ourselves hanging on to others, more out of desperation than love.

All relationships have this egocentric element, but when our needs overshadow our celebration of another, the love is as a car looking for an outlet on a cul-de-sac.

๑๑

Love lives on hope, and dies when hope is dead;
It is a flame which sinks for lack of fuel.
PIERRE CORNEILLE

Are you intimate with yourself?

You may recall in the introduction of this book I described my life upheaval of some years ago. At that time, and long before it, I would have considered myself a person who had no problems with intimacy. I could tell those close to me that I loved them and was comfortable sharing my feelings with others. Part of what I think led to my despair, however, was that I was never really intimate with myself. I never quieted my mind long enough to know what was going on inside of me. I thought I was doing so, but I can see now that I wasn't.

How do you go about being self-intimate? I have two suggestions. First, be still in body and spirit. The knowledge you need will float to the surface when you stop hurrying around. Second, find a wise person (i.e., one who does not have an answer to every problem; look for silence in your sages) and don't just talk, but listen.

@@

Intimacy begins with oneself.
It does no good to try to find intimacy with friends,
lovers and family if you are starting out
from alienation and division within yourself.
THOMAS MOORE

How do you envision spiritual peace?

I suspect that one reason people buy and read self-help books is that they are in pain of one sort or another and want to find a way out of it. The problem is, there is no way to get out of pain but to go through it. People who have worked at cultivating a peaceful spirit still experience as much pain as everyone else, but they come to recognize pain as a part of life's process. They don't run from suffering, but embrace it and learn from it.

◎◎

Weeping washes the face.
HINDUSTANI PROVERB

Are you willing to be a fool?

A common excuse for not giving money to panhandlers is that they'll just use the money for booze. "So," we say nobly, "to give them money is to enable their destruction." Although there is often some truth to this rationalization, I suspect that what really bugs people is the prospect of being deceived, of being made the fool.

Love and compassion often demand that we turn from earthly wisdom and risk looking stupid. If we are to love all of our brothers and sisters, we need to act, and actions lead to failures and embarrassments. No matter. Love, even foolish love, is a wisdom in and of itself.

@@

It is impossible to love and be wise.
FRANCIS BACON

*Do you learn from your pain
as you work through it?*

When we look back at difficult times in our lives, we sometimes forget to give thanks for what those times have taught us. Imagine how much more peaceful your life can be if you recognize the importance of suffering not after you've gone through it, but *as* you're going through it. The sense of desperation you feel during suffering can be buffered by the knowledge that you will grow from and gain wisdom through the experience.

⊚⊚

We cannot learn without pain.
ARISTOTLE

*When you've been emotionally injured,
do you give yourself time to hurt and to heal?*

One common way to respond to loss is to get busy.
The idea is that, if we have lots of things to do, we
won't dwell on our suffering. Although there's some
merit to this philosophy, by and large it deprives us of
what we must go through to heal. Spiritual peace isn't
attained by bouncing back quickly, but by both suffering and healing *fully*.

☺☺

*We are healed of a suffering
only by experiencing it to the full.*
MARCEL PROUST

Can you spot a spiritual crisis
when you're in one?

One blessing of the peace journey is that it provides a container for our suffering. We know that life is joyous *and* painful, and we stop engaging in the fantasy that someday when we get rich all our tough times will be past.

Once we accept the reality of spiritual crises, we can know peace in the midst of struggle. We actually begin to appreciate the process of enduring loss to make room for growth.

◎◎

It is in this darkness, when there is nothing left in us that can please or comfort our own minds, when we seem to be useless and worthy of all contempt, when we seem to have failed, when we seem to be destroyed and devoured, it is then that the deep and secret selfishness that is too close for us to identify is stripped away from our souls. It is in this darkness that we find true liberty. It is in this abandonment that we are made strong. This is the night which empties us and makes us pure.

THOMAS MERTON

*Despite your best efforts,
do you see the demonstration of emotions
as a weakness?*

How many times have you overheard or taken part in a conversation like the one below?

"Hey, did you hear that Phil died?"

"Oh, God, no. That's too bad. How's his wife holding up?"

"Not so good. I saw her at the funeral home last night. She's pretty broken up."

My question is, why should anybody be "holding up" when a loved one dies? Although crying is pretty fashionable these days (a television interview just isn't viewed as successful unless the interviewee gets all choked up), displays of emotion are perceived as weak and uncouth.

Let go of the Victorian notion that feelings should be kept inside.

☙❧

*Never look down on somebody
unless you're helping him up.*
JESSE JACKSON

*Have you forgiven yourself for the pain
you've caused yourself?*

When we think of healing and forgiveness, we most often think of what other people, or mere chance, have done to us. We generally forget to forgive ourselves for our mistakes and heal from the pain we've inflicted upon ourselves. Unfortunately, we're much more willing to forgive others than we are to forgive ourselves. We must cultivate the capacity to be merciful to ourselves.

☙❧

Heal us, Lord, and we shall be healed.
FROM A JEWISH PRAYER

Are you ever in emotional pain and don't know why?

I believe that most of us carry around pain from past incidents that we've never allowed ourselves to fully encounter. For this reason, on any given day, we might feel inexplicably sad or depressed. Although we may never learn exactly which event still causes us pain, we can acknowledge the legitimacy of our suffering and hope that it might teach us something someday.

◎◎

It would be great to understand pain in all its meanings.
PETER MERE LATHAM

Are you a fun person?

Central to spiritual peace is the ability to relax, to be spontaneous, to have fun. It's no accident that the Buddha depicted in many a statue has a silly grin on his face or is in the middle of a big belly laugh. The most peaceful people I know love to laugh and have a good time.

Jesus in his Sermon on the Mount preaches idleness:
"Consider the lilies of the field. . . ."
Jehovah, the bearded and angry god,
gave his worshippers the supreme example
of ideal laziness: after six days of work
he rested for all eternity.
PAUL LAGARGUE

Is your home a happy place?

It's pretty difficult to be at peace if you don't like to be at home. Your house should be a place where you feel content, where you can have a good time and not worry about wrecking something all the time. Sure, nobody wants to have grape juice stains on the sofa, but if your furniture, or any object for that matter, is more important than the person using it, then your priorities are goofed up. When given the choice, sacrifice the "perfect" house and create what Germans call *gemutlichkeit*—warmth, hospitality, homeyness, and probably a few stains.

@@

It takes a heap o' livin' in a house t' make it home.
EDGAR ALBERT GUEST

Do you get angry when your plans fall apart?

Are you a controlling person? If so, you may have trouble letting your hair down on a moment's notice. You may also get very attached to whatever plans you make, and when those plans get threatened, you become angry. Letting go of the controls is difficult, but it's essential to spiritual peace. You have to learn to jump in water with your good clothes on, to go for a walk in the snow even though you had your heart set on going to the movies, and to picnic in your living room when it's cold and rainy.

๏๏

Some of the most rewarding and beautiful moments
of a friendship happen in the unforeseen open
spaces between planned activities. It is important
that you allow these spaces to exist.
CHRISTINE LEEFELDT
AND ERNEST CALLENBACH

Are you able to make your work fun?

Let's face it, some of us have jobs that aren't fun; however, we can make our work more bearable by losing ourselves in the present moment. If we think of our labor as a prayer, something to be done well, then the task at hand becomes a meditation, a reaching out of our talents. Work doesn't have to be complete drudgery if we adjust our attitudes toward it.

∾

"Mr. Gandhi," a Western journalist asked him once,
"you have been working at least fifteen hours
a day, every day, for almost fifty years.
Don't you think it's about time you took a vacation?"
"Why?" Gandhi said. "I am always on vacation."

FROM *GANDHI THE MAN*
BY EKNATH EASWARAN

Is having fun a priority for you?

For many of us, having fun is something we'll do if we have time, only after all our work is finished. Maybe the world has to be this way, but I think God wants us to spend as much time playing as working. Why would God create a stunningly gorgeous world, plop us down in it, and then say, "Please work extremely hard and have fun only if you can spare the time"? I believe that God expects us to have a good time. Pleasure should be a priority.

@

If a man insisted always on being serious,
and never allowed himself a bit of fun
and relaxation, he would go mad or become
unstable without knowing it.
HERODOTUS

So what's holding you back?

As I write this, my daughter Elena is at a magical moment in her life. She hasn't yet filled her satchel with silly and unreasonable fears. She's not into boys, so she hasn't sustained her first love lacerations. And since the idea of mortality hasn't hit home, she dances through her days.

When I watch Elena play, I realize there's no way to quite get back to that time once we've grown up. Almost every day, however, chances to be children again crowd around us, and we overlook them: running with a child; having a good, pure belly laugh with a friend; dancing in your living room with the curtains open; standing on the porch in the middle of winter with your bathrobe and breathing the fresh air; playing tug-of-war with a dog. Such moments are gifts, gateways to tastes of freedom.

ᥫᩭ

Like a kite
Cut from the string,
Lightly the soul of my youth
Has taken flight.
ISHIKAWA TAKUBOKU

What's your purpose in life?

Let's experiment with a paradigm shift. What would happen to your decision-making processes if you somehow found out that God wants, more than anything else, for you to enjoy life and that the things preventing us from pleasure are the fault of humanity and not God? In difficult times, therefore, you might say to yourself, "God doesn't want me to suffer. God wants me to be content and at peace." Regardless of what we're doing, I believe that God's will for our lives is not pain and toil, but happiness and health.

◎◎

The rule of my life is to make business a pleasure,
and pleasure my business.
AARON BURR

Are you simply existing?

Harriet, my late grandmother, could be stubborn. When she was seventy-five years old, she would drive across the country alone, despite the family's objections. At eighty-three she made a trip to Florida just after a considerable illness, and while there she had a major stroke which eventually took her life.

Although this trip may have hastened Harriet's end, I applaud her determination to keep living. In her last years, she somehow knew that her death was not far off, and she refused to sit still just to squeeze a few more months out of life. She lived—even as she bravely prepared to die. The year before her death she gave away all of her old photographs, had a booklet of her best recipes printed up for the family, and gave people possessions she knew they appreciated. All of this she did not with morbidity or exaggerated emotion, but with simplicity and joy. Even as Harriet was preparing to die, she *lived,* and in so doing showered life and dignity on those she loved.

@@

I would rather be ashes than dust! . . .
The proper function of a man is to live, not to exist.
I shall not waste my days in trying to prolong them.
I shall use my time.
JACK LONDON

*Do you find that the harder you try to make
things go your way, the worse things turn out?*

Sometimes life tries to tell us that we're swimming
against the current, but most of us don't listen. As a
culture we revere people who are stubborn, who don't
take no for an answer, who pursue their dreams even
when all odds are against them. The problem is, we
seem to hear only of those who fulfill their dreams,
not of those who fail. Actually what our culture should
revere is discernment and insight. There are times
when we ought to ignore the naysayers, but if all people and events are telling us "nay," then maybe we
need to listen. The key is having enough objectivity
and self-awareness to recognize when attempts to
control matters are excessive. When we use too much
force to make things go our way, we usually end up
hurting ourselves and others.

@@

The greatest griefs are those we cause ourselves.
SOPHOCLES

Do you know what will make you happy in the future?

We think we're pretty smart here on the doorstep of the twenty-first century. Sending a person to the moon isn't an issue anymore; we did that more than twenty-five years ago. We also know that we could feed the entire world if we really wanted to. So why, if we're so smart, are so many people suffering, not to mention dying in wars and famine? The answer is that, despite all of our scientific knowledge, we're the last to know what's good for our planet. We're probably also the last to know what's best for ourselves. My own experience certainly bears this out. The things I used to think would make me happy haven't, and the things I never cared about are the joy of my life today. Is this true in your life? Perhaps you don't know what will make you happy. Perhaps God is the only one who knows what you need.

⚭

Where is the wisdom we have lost in knowledge?
Where is the knowledge we have lost in information?
T. S. ELIOT

Are you afraid of the unknown?

Although the unknown can be frightening, there's a positive side to not knowing what's ahead: you're not responsible for what you can't predict. Life's lighter somehow when you look into mysteries with a fundamental trust in the goodness of creation and the gentleness of God. The unknown then becomes a darkness you can look into with a smile.

◎◎

I said to a man who stood at the gate of the year: "Give me a light that I may tread safely into the unknown." And he replied, "Go out into the darkness and put your hand into the hand of God. That shall be to you better than a light and safer than a known way."
MINNIE L. HASKINS

*Do you wish that the circumstances
of your life would change?*

If you are presently in horrible circumstances, you are probably right to wish for change; however, for those of us who have no particular reason to be unhappy, constantly wishing for change is harmful. It means we're spending too much time thinking about the sour spots in our lives and not enough time celebrating the sweet spots. Changes in our situations won't make us happy. *We* must change if we're to join the cosmic dance.

@@

. . . be transformed by the renewing of your minds.
ROMANS 12:2

What is loneliness?

When people are lonely, those of us who are not offer lots of great advice. "Why don't you do volunteer work?" we say. "That way you could meet people." We also tell lonely people to keep busy so that they don't have time to dwell on being alone.

These suggestions have some merit, but they don't acknowledge the roots of loneliness: a feeling of separation from the Divine; and a hunger not just for the presence of others, but for *intimacy*. In not understanding why people are lonely, we offer shallow-minded counsel that's about as wise as telling folks to eat borscht as a remedy for cataracts. Silly!

Because we long for intimacy with others and with God, we feel isolated, even when in a crowd. It's fitting, then, that the people who seldom seem lonely to me are the nuns I know. I don't want to romanticize here, but some sisters, even those who live alone, are the opposite of lonely, if that is possible. When they enter a room, they bring with them a crowd of joy, which comes from a heart always open to the Divine.

@

In solitude the lonely man is eaten up by himself,
among the crowds by many.
FRIEDRICH NIETZSCHE

*Do you shape your experiences
as they are shaping you?*

Joseph Merrick, the Elephant Man of Victorian England (his name was not "John," by the way, but "Joseph"), was terribly disfigured, exploited, and brutalized. When late in life he found a home in the London Hospital under the care of his physician and friend Frederick Treves, the world came to know Merrick as thoughtful, talented, and most of all, kind. Merrick obviously had the ability not simply to be shaped by his experiences, but to shape them as well. He shaped years of abuse into compassion.

We can do the same thing. In the silent, peaceful pockets of our days we can prayerfully, slowly turn sorrow into an outpouring of love and understanding. We can participate in our creation and re-creation.

◈◈

*Experience is not what happens to a man.
It is what a man does with what happens to him.*
ALDOUS HUXLEY

Do you know your place?

Regardless of how much our spirits grow toward peace, there are always those moments when we have to face our personal demons. We lay awake at 3 A.M. and, in the darkness, feel in our muscles and bones those things we tell nobody, our secret sufferings and longings, our angers and truths. Or maybe we feel this dull ache of our humanity while we suppose we ought to be happy, like when we're sitting on a blanket in the sun and breeze, talking with loved ones.

Although no one likes to suffer, it's possible to find healing when our wounds are exposed. Rather than lament the fact that we're miserable, we can reflect on the power of the Divine to turn pain into wisdom and compassion. And we can admit that God's still, small voice (and only that voice), which resides within and around us, gives us light and life at those moments when we most know our brokenness.

@@

Closer is He than breathing,
and nearer than hands and feet.
ALFRED, LORD TENNYSON

Do you have faith?

Although it's not necessary to embrace any particular religious belief for this book to be useful to you, it is necessary to have faith in something. My faith is in a loving, compassionate God. Yours might be in the random beauty of the cosmos or in the logical order of earth. The important belief to hold is that there is a wisdom and love that is ever in the process of making things right. The world may not be right today, but if you open yourself to this love (I call this love "God"), you will move in the direction of peace and goodness, and this is the best thing you can do to right the world.

@@

Nothing in life is more wonderful than faith—the one great moving force which we can neither weigh in the balance nor test in the crucible.
SIR WILLIAM OSLER

Can you be sad and at peace at the same time?

As this book suggests more than once, happiness and spiritual peace aren't synonymous. We all go through unavoidable periods of suffering: loved ones die; the cruelty of the world disappoints us; those close to us engage in self-destructive behavior. During such times of unhappiness, it is helpful to remember that we **can** be sad and at peace at the same time.

Nobody likes suffering, but it is woven into our days. The key, of course, is to turn away from unnecessary suffering. When we can't do so, we need to enter fully into our pain and remember that God is with us every moment of every day. If *we* remain present to God, we can be at peace as we wait for healing.

@@

He who has courage and faith
will never perish in misery!
ANNE FRANK

Do your decisions always have to make sense?

One legitimate consideration we often neglect when we make decisions is faith. I'm not talking here about reacting to "gut" instinct, but about a deep and quiet certainty of what we ought to do. For example, we might feel a strong compulsion to give fifty dollars to a friend who's in trouble even when we're pretty short ourselves. It makes little sense to do so, yet we hear that interior, wordless voice that helps us know what to do.

The more I live, the more faith I have that God resides in those gentle, merciful, courageous words we hear without hearing and accept without understanding. The people I know who keep an ear inclined toward this voice are teachers of peace for me.

@@

. . . we walk by faith, not by sight.
2 CORINTHIANS 5:7

Do you feel alone?

We live in a world without worldly promises. We don't know if there is some divine plan for our earthly lives. There is no guarantee that everything we depend upon for our comfort will not be gone tomorrow (and any faith that claims otherwise is lying). One of the few guarantees we have is stated in the quotation below. We are not alone, and we are not forgotten.

◎◎

I will never leave you or forsake you.
HEBREWS 13:5

Are you an energetic and upbeat person?

Many of us walk around in a blue funk for no reason. We cultivate in ourselves a negative attitude and a somber disposition. If you're being downbeat and you're not suffering, grieving, or clinically depressed, try to make optimism and vitality your *modus operandi*. You'd be surprised how much more gratifying and exciting life can be if you simply make up your mind to be positive, energetic, full of hope.

෩

If you be not ill, be not ill-like.
SCOTTISH PROVERB

Do you have a healthy passion?

For centuries numerous venerated religious thinkers have told us to reject earthly pleasures because catering to the passions of the flesh takes our attention away from God. Perhaps it is a reflection of the time in which I live, but I believe it is possible to be a full participant in the physical life and still make a growing, legitimate peace journey.

In fact, I think healthy passions, sexual and non-sexual ones, are a positive force. Your spirit's home is glad to enjoy your mate's skin against yours; to taste good food; to ride a bike and feel wind wrap itself around you; to celebrate the overflowing of this earthly life.

People seeking peace don't need to reject passions; moreover, we're obligated to seek out and accept divine gifts.

᠑᠑

One declaims endlessly against the passions;
one imputes all of man's suffering to them.
One forgets that they are also the source
of all his pleasures.
DENIS DIDEROT

Are you a couch potato?

Did you know that there really is a natural high? When you elevate your heart rate for twenty minutes or so, the brain releases endorphins, which act like nature's morphine. For several hours after strenuous exercise, most people feel energetic, yet calm. If you don't exercise, you're not permitting yourself the natural stress relief that facilitates peace of mind and spirit. So get off the couch and take a walk or dance or lose at tennis. Be alive!

@@

The plow that works is always shiny.
GREEK PROVERB

Can you motivate yourself to do things you don't really want to do?

The tasks we face with dread often prove, in the end, to be helpful and gratifying. Exercise is a good example. Exerting yourself physically seems as though it would make you tired, but, in fact, it makes you strong. My mother, who has arthritis, knows this. I try to get her to a track near my house as often as possible, and when she finishes walking her one or two laps, she says that she actually feels better physically and mentally than before she walked. There's magic in exercise.

෨෧

Would you live with ease, do what you ought,
and not what you please.
BENJAMIN FRANKLIN

Do you break large goals into small goals?

Part of my job as a college instructor is to help students learn how to manage their workloads. One technique (not a new one for sure) that I often discuss is breaking large goals into smaller ones. For example, a student will be staggered by the amount of work necessary to complete a research project that's due in a few weeks. The first thing I'll recommend is that she forget about the whole project, but just stop by the library today to see what books are available on the subject. Then tomorrow, go again and see what periodical articles she can find. And so on. The prospect of a large goal is suddenly manageable when the student focuses on a series of small tasks rather than an overwhelming totality.

Although ultimate goals need to be kept in mind, breaking them into "day-sized" chunks is healthy and conducive to spiritual peace.

@@

Many strokes overthrow the tallest oaks.
JOHN LYLY

When was the last time you physically challenged yourself?

If you haven't exercised in a long time, you might think that your body just isn't capable of doing the things it used to do. In my home town of Erie, Pennsylvania, Barb Filutze probably thought the same thing. Barb started running after having kids and giving up a hearty smoking habit. Now in her early fifties, she is, according to *Runner's World* magazine, one of the best women runners *in the world* for her age. Who would have thought that possible?

What's possible for you?

@@

Above all, challenge yourself.
You may well surprise yourself at what strengths
you have, what you can accomplish.
CECILE M. SPRINGER

How old are you?

A couple of years ago I was standing in line at a drinking fountain before a 13.1-mile footrace. Before me stood a guy who was obviously in his late fifties or early sixties. He was bald, but had a lean, muscular body—put me to shame. After he got his drink, I heard a guy behind me say that the man was in his mid-seventies. This half-marathon was a jog around the block for him, for he frequently ran fifty-mile races.

Stories like this generally make us feel inadequate, but I mention this man because I think we sometimes allow "realities" to limit us. If it were possible to truly forget your age, for example, how old would you say you are? If you could forget your weight, would you be likely to call yourself fat?

I'm not suggesting here that we completely ignore facts, rather that we watch for those moments when we're tempted to buy into unnecessary realities.

@@

How old would you be
if you didn't know how old you was?
SATCHEL PAIGE

Do you believe you can be happy?

Life is often a self-fulfilling prophecy: if you expect things to go poorly, they probably will. For example, if you have children and believe that bedtime is going to be frustrating, it probably will be. Chances are, you will look for reasons to be angry and thus confirm your fears; however, if you are confident that you can keep your cool and deal creatively with conflict, you'll be more likely to succeed. The same is true with happiness. People who walk around saying that happiness is not in the cards for them appear to attract bad luck. In truth, their luck is generally no worse than anyone else's, but they tend to focus on their misery and habitually put themselves in positions where bad luck is sure to strike. On the other hand, people who assume that they ought to be happy usually find much to appreciate. I know that I risk over-generalizing here, but my experience is that most people (not all, but most) create their own joy and despair.

☺☺

You have to believe in happiness
or happiness never comes.
DOUGLAS MALLOCH

Do you believe in yourself?

As with the previous question, this one points toward self-fulfilling prophecies. When you assume that you will fail, you create images of doubt and fear in your mind that you keep watching over and over. By the time you're faced with a challenge, you've witnessed your own failure so many times that you almost automatically act out your own vision. In short, you defeat yourself. On the other hand, if you purposely develop mental pictures of yourself doing well, you empower yourself to feel confident and to succeed.

◎◉

Believe in yourself. Have faith in your abilities.
NORMAN VINCENT PEALE

Are you a positive thinker?

Most situations have roughly the same number of positives and negatives. Why not choose to dwell on the good things rather than the bad? Are you broke? Consider the lean times as a chance to learn how good you can become at getting something for nothing (e.g., coupons and sales). Of course, such positive thinking takes energy and determination, and if taken to extremes, it can turn to simple denial, but looking for the hidden benefits in bad circumstances helps to buffer pain and give meaning to suffering.

◎◎

Make a crutch of your cross.
ENGLISH PROVERB

Are you complimentary and encouraging to others?

One of the best ways of learning to be a positive thinker is to be a source of optimism to others. Sure, you don't want to be the sort of bonehead who always walks around telling people to make lemonade when life gives them lemons, but you can create around yourself a spirit of goodwill and hope. You can tell co-workers how much you appreciate their hard work, encourage friends to develop their talents, and help everyone around you to concentrate on possibilities rather than obstacles. Let people come to know you as uplifting. When you walk into a room, people should feel a little happier and healthier than they did a few minutes before.

@@

Never lose a chance of saying a kind word.
WILLIAM MAKEPEACE THACKERAY

Do you bring out the best in others?

The peace journey can help us see people in a new way. We cut back on criticizing and teasing others and may begin to form friendships with people nobody seems to get along with. This is because the peaceful person sees beyond the flaws to the potential. Perhaps this sounds elitist, but in my experience peaceful people bring out the best in those they love. They encourage, support, and uplift. The effort to abide in God's peace, then, can change bystanders, who see themselves not as they are, but as they can be.

This journey you are on is not just for you, but also for those you love.

☯

*If you treat an individual as he is, he will stay as he is,
but if you treat him as if he were what he
ought to be and could be, he will become
what he ought to be and what he could be.*
GOETHE

Do you sometimes get lost in self-pity?

Sometimes is the key word. When a loved one dies, when you lose a job, when you get dumped by the person of your dreams, you're entitled to some self-pity. If you get to feeling sorry for yourself too often, though, then you're concentrating on past difficulties rather than on what you can do to improve the future.

◎◎

Never feel self-pity, the most destructive emotion there is. How awful to be caught up in the terrible squirrel cage of self.
MILLICENT FENWICK

Do you live life?

When you're down in the dumps or fearful, you're not living life. Take a vow to let yourself be crazy, to laugh, to dance, to take chances. Don't let the rain stop you from playing a game of catch. Don't let the fear of cracking a note keep you from singing. Don't let people who always have a crummy thing to say keep you from chasing a dream. Go after life.

✺

You don't get to choose how you're going to die.
Or when. You can only decide how you're going to live.
Now.
JOAN BAEZ

Do you take advantage of "killed" time?

Think of how many times a day you let your time get killed: waiting at red lights, standing in line at the grocery store, watching food cook on the stove. I once read somewhere that we spend on average two years of our lives waiting in line.

As Henry David Thoreau suggests below, killing time diminishes us. Worse than that, I would argue that the ways in which we kill time are unhealthy. For example, in the store we get angry at having to wait even though we have no control over the situation. Wouldn't we be much happier if we gave a purpose to that time of waiting. Relaxation is the easiest thing to do when you have empty time on your hands. All you need to do is say to yourself, "Instead of getting impatient, I can use this time to rest." Close your eyes for a moment, take a few deep, cleansing breaths, tune in to where your body is tense, and relax those muscles. In this way, you can turn a time of stress into one of refreshment.

@@

As if you could kill time without injuring eternity.
HENRY DAVID THOREAU

What is poverty?

When we think of poverty, we tend to think of those who don't have enough money to pay for the necessities in life, but there is another devastating kind of poverty—poverty of the soul. The words below by Geoffrey Chaucer are difficult to read because they're fourteenth-century English, but understanding their meaning is paramount to achieving spiritual peace. Chaucer's Wife of Bath asks us who is poorer, the impoverished person who wants little or the rich person who still wants a lot. You decide.

◎◎

Whoso that halt him paid of his poverte
I holde him riche al hadde he nat a sherte.
He that coveiteth is a poor wight,
For he wolde han that is nat in his might;
But he that nought hath, ne coveiteth have
Is riche, although we holde him but a knave.
GEOFFREY CHAUCER

Is your life cluttered with commitments?

Sometimes the sheer number of tasks we have to do is enough to keep us from feeling peaceful. The old adage "less is more" is really true. It's better to do a few things well than to do a whole bunch of things poorly.

◎◎

Our life is frittered away by detail. . . .
Simplicity, simplicity, simplicity!
I say, let our affairs be as two or three,
and not a hundred or a thousand . . .
simplicity of life and elevation of purpose.
HENRY DAVID THOREAU

Are you filled with want?

A popular bumper sticker these days reads, "The one who dies with the most toys wins." Actually, it ought to read, "The one who dies with the most toys has a big thing for toys and is pretty selfish." The more objects you want to possess, the farther you are from the cosmic dance. "Want's" appetite is insatiable, so rather than chase everything you want, gain a measure of rationality regarding what you want. Focus on getting rid of want rather than on feeding it with hors d'oeuvre after hors d'oeuvre.

◎◎

Manifest plainness,
Embrace simplicity,
Reduce selfishness,
Have few desires.
LAO-TZU

Is your spirit gray?

If people could see the face of your spirit, how would they describe it? Are the lines of this face lifted upward, as if anticipating some great joy? Or are the eyes of this face cupped by pale bruises that have seen mostly pain and expect to see nothing more?

With our faces of flesh, we don't have many natural ways of altering our appearance. With our spiritual faces, however, we can ask for and receive smooth skin and lips that can't help singing.

@@

> *I ask no dream, no prophet ecstasies,*
> *No sudden rending of the veil of clay,*
> *No angel visitant, no opening skies,*
> *But take the dimness of my soul away.*
> GEORGE CROLY

Are you concerned about being fashionable?

If you're still reading this book, chances are you're not awfully worried about following the latest fads, but if you are, you should know that fashion can be a barrier to peace. If you're constantly thinking of how you're looking, you're not giving yourself fully to the present moment. Some of the most beautiful people I know are the dorkiest dressers. Some of the most gentle are unable to afford fine clothing and are always a decade behind. Who really cares? A good and noble soul clothes itself.

◎◎

Consider the lilies of the field, how they grow;
they neither toil nor spin, yet I tell you,
Solomon in all his glory was not clothed
like one of these.
MATTHEW 6:28–29

Are you comfortable being yourself?

If you're concerned about what others think of you, you're losing out on the beauty of the present moment. People are always going to judge one another, and that's too bad. When people judge you, accept that you can't control what others think. Live freely and fully who you are (provided, of course, that who you are isn't harmful to yourself and others) and leave those who are inclined to condemn you to their bitter satisfaction.

☺☺

I want to be seen here in my simple, natural, ordinary fashion, without straining or artifice. . . .
MICHEL EYQUEM DE MONTAIGNE

Are you satisfied with your body?

Everyone's body has flaws: blemished skin, a roll of fat, discolored teeth. Imperfection is the norm. The question is, are you reasonably happy with your body. You won't move toward spiritual peace unless you either come to terms with yourself physically or take action to improve your body. Naturally, I'm not talking about having every little wart removed, but about developing a sense of ease with your body, which is God's creation.

۞

If anything is sacred the human body is sacred.
WALT WHITMAN

Can you see the sacred in the commonplace?

We see thousands of images every day that reveal the presence of God, but we look right past them. The cosmic dance takes place on wet grass, and nobody wears shoes. Experience God in what you see but fail to notice: the quirky way children run, the sun rising over rooftops, your own hands.

☺☺

I wish that life should not be cheap, but sacred.
I wish the days to be as centuries, loaded, fragrant.
RALPH WALDO EMERSON

Are you open to the lessons of nature?

Many valuable and useful lessons are right outside our windows, and the tuition is free. Watching a bird build a nest can teach patience. The color of fall leaves speaks of the beauty possible in growing old. A walk around the block can make you wise if you watch and listen.

ꮺ

Come forth into the light of things,
Let Nature be your teacher.
WILLIAM WORDSWORTH

Are you aware of the process as well as the product of your labors?

Many of us have responsibilities that don't seem very beautiful or important, yet it is the honesty and grace of the effort that ennobles labor, not the product. Consider sweeping a floor, for example. Silly as it may sound, if you take away the broom and the purpose of the task, you might well call what remains a dance.

☺☺

Honest labor bears a lovely face.
THOMAS DEKKER

What does the face of God look like?

If we acknowledge that our bodies, nature, and labor are all creations of God and, therefore, sacred, we must also acknowledge the holiness of our fellow human beings. Our world is full of people who need love and care. Some need food. Some need a smile and a hello. Some need understanding. All need love. Look into the face of every person you see today. See the face of God.

◎◎

Being unwanted, unloved, uncared for, forgotten by everybody, I think that is a much greater hunger, a much greater poverty than the person who has nothing to eat. . . . We must find each other.

MOTHER TERESA

Do you allow ugliness to detract from beauty?

Beneath the ugliness you can often find beauty. A dirty, oily pair of hands seems ugly until you remember that those hands repaired your car. One of the most hideous looking persons of all time, Joseph Merrick, the Elephant Man, gave Victorian England the chance to be charitable and reminded them of how fortunate one is to have a reasonably healthy body, food enough to survive, and a warm place to sleep. Although Merrick's contorted skeleton still stands in the London Hospital as a model of physical deformity, his life has been the subject of an inspiring film, a play, and several books. Not bad for a person so ugly people ran screaming at the sight of him.

❧

Advice for a teenage daughter—
five inexpensive beauty hints:
For attractive lips, speak words of kindness;
for lovely eyes, seek out the good in people;
for a slim figure, share your food with the hungry;
for beautiful hair, let a child run his fingers through it
once a day. And, for poise, walk with the knowledge
that you will never walk alone.
SAM LEVENSON

Are you being ripped from the mountainside?

Ken, a good friend of mine, goes on retreats to Zen monasteries from time to time. During one retreat, in the course of meditating for more than ten hours per day, Ken went to the master to talk about a problem. The lotus position was hurting him, and he didn't know what to do.

"The pain is ripping me from the mountainside," Ken said.

"So jump," the master replied.

Ken went back to meditating, and this time instead of fighting the pain, he entered into it fully. Eventually, rather than being an entirely unpleasant experience, the pain became a sort of white-hot world that surrounded Ken.

I know you're probably thinking, "Ken should've stretched his leg or gone for a walk." Half of me agrees, but the other half sees a lesson here: sometimes the best way to achieve inner peace is to surrender to distractions, for they might be trying to teach us something. Ken gained a greater understanding of pain; who knows what we might learn.

೦⊚

Destiny grants us our wishes, but in its own way,
in order to give us something beyond our wishes.
GOETHE

Do you like a good mystery?

We've all heard people say that they'd prefer bad news to no news at all, that the agony is in not knowing. For the person seeking peace, mysteries, especially big ones (e.g., What happens when we die?) must become sacred. We must learn to wrap ourselves up in and befriend the unknown, not to fight against it.

@@

It is good to love the unknown.
CHARLES LAMB

Do people know what you stand for?

Have you ever tried to keep something secret? Recall for a moment the unpleasant feelings associated with secrets—the sinking feeling of being discovered, muscles clenching at the thought of the consequences. Phooey. Better to live openly, letting those you meet know right from the beginning who you are. This is not to suggest, however, that you should spill your guts out to each person you meet upon introduction. The point is, you can't be at peace when you're on the run from yourself and others.

@@

It's important to let people know what you stand for.
It's equally important that they know
what you won't stand for.
B. BADER

Are you just in dealing with others?

Folks who have spent some time on the peace path don't generally have problems being fair in dealing with others; in fact, we can be too lenient, if that is possible. For example, as a college English teacher, I had a habit in the past of bending over backwards to pass students who I knew could do the work, but were lazy. I would think to myself, "Why penalize them because they're young and foolish?" The problem was, most of these students ended up dropping out before long because they really didn't want to be in college in the first place.

Was I just in dealing with these students? In the end, I don't think so. What I did was permit a behavior other people weren't going to put up with, and so I sent a false message. Now I still try to be loving, forgiving, but *fair*. If students don't follow the rules, and if they don't have a compelling reason for falling short, then they fail. The realization I came to is that being just may be unpleasant, but it's necessary.

◎◎

It is impossible to be just if one is not generous.
JOSEPH ROUX

What is hospitality?

In the gospel according to Saint Matthew, Jesus tells those listening to love their enemies, "for if you love those who love you, what reward do you have? Do not even the tax collectors do the same?" (Even in those days, the IRS had a reputation.)

What is said here about love might also be said about hospitality. How can we call ourselves good hosts when we welcome only those close to us into our homes? We can't. Hospitality lives when we *wel come,* not just put up with, but welcome, those whose behavior we might not appreciate, whose presence puts a wrinkle in things.

As people of peace, we need to *be,* as much as we are able, the face of *agape,* the unconditional love of God. That requires costly hospitality, not the cheap kind we all claim to possess.

❧

You ought to make welcome the present guest,
and send forth the one who wishes to go.
HOMER

*Do you sometimes feel overwhelmed
and paralyzed by the number of
problems in the world?*

Just as it is important to make personal priorities, it is also vital to prioritize your relationship with the world. Although we're all obligated to help end suffering, one person can't help everybody, but one person can help another person. Reaching out through volunteerism is a way of acting upon the sorrow we feel for all those who need our help.

@

*One cannot weep for the entire world.
It is beyond human strength.
One must choose.*
JEAN ANOUILH

Do you have peace words?

There are moments when we don't have the luxury to process information as it comes in before we must react to it. We might have to deal with a friend's unexpected sorrow, a stranger's angry outburst, a child's profound fear. At such times, to minimize our own and others' suffering, it's good to have words of peace in our minds that rise to the surface and remind us of our call to accept the Divine presence and offer it to those around us.

I use the phrase "God's peace" when I'm swept away by harmful situations. The words calm my body and soothe my mind so that I can act as an instrument of love.

☺☺

Words are a small change of thought.
JULES RENARD

Are kindness and love your top priorities?

When we get into the business of setting priorities, we sometimes forget the priority that cancels out all the rest: "love one another." This beautiful rule aggravates those of us who like to lead neat, well-organized lives. Love asks us to ditch our agenda for the day to spend time with a friend who needs our presence. Love calls us to put money into our struggling church's offering plate when we'd rather buy one more toy for ourselves. If your plans in life do not often get snagged on the demands of love, then you're probably sticking to your plan more than you ought to.

⊚⊚

That best portion of a good man's life,
His little, nameless, unremembered acts
Of kindness and of love.
WILLIAM WORDSWORTH

Can you understand
without understanding?

In "The Yellow Wallpaper," a short story by Charlotte Perkins Gilman, the narrator is driven insane by the inability of those around her to validate her severe depression and her need for contact with others. Throughout the story her husband, a physician, talks to her as if she were a child and insists that she receive complete rest—no activity, no visitors. Clearly, nobody in the story *understands* what the narrator is going through, and because they don't understand, they don't acknowledge her feelings. In the end, their "cure" exacerbates her condition.

One meaning of "understand" is to mentally process and make meaning of something. Another meaning, which I saw on a colleague's bulletin board, is "to stand under"—to support. It is possible to recognize another person's feelings and offer sympathy without fully comprehending what the person is going through. Even when we don't understand, we can be messengers of peace by standing under.

๑๑

In daily life we never understand each other,
neither complete clairvoyance
nor complete confessional exists.
E. M. FORSTER

Are you able to do without?

If we're hungry, most of us can hop in the car and within twenty minutes or so have a fully cooked meal. Computers bring information to us in seconds. Many of the things people used to have to work hard for are easily obtained nowadays, so much so that it's difficult to deny ourselves anything. Yet the person who seeks peace must learn to live with want. Living through longing teaches us that we're usually starving for something much larger and more fundamental than food or possessions. Through the struggles of self-denial, we begin to uncover the true sources of the hunger we're trying to satisfy in the wrong way.

೦⊚

Nihil nimis.
[Nothing in excess.]
ANONYMOUS

What is plenty?

On Thanksgiving, tables across the United States are covered with so many platters of food that there's hardly room for people to set their plates. And so we give thanks by seeing how much we can eat—rather like a kid saying thanks to her or his parents for the use of a car by putting 10,000 miles a month on it. Wouldn't the parent rather the kid showed appreciation by using the car wisely?

❦

*They are as sick that surfeit with too much
as they that starve with nothing.*
WILLIAM SHAKESPEARE

Do you take pleasure in gossiping about people's shortcomings and weaknesses?

Talking others down brings with it slightly malicious pleasure, but such talk always does violence to the speaker. The next time you find yourself in the midst of trashing somebody, stop and ask yourself why you're doing so. Are you trying to feel pleased with yourself by bruising another? When you finish speaking thoughtlessly, pause and take inventory of your soul. Don't you feel diminished? Are there any redeeming qualities in mean-spirited gossip?

⊗⊗

What you don't see with your eyes,
don't witness with your mouth.
JEWISH PROVERB

Do you love your enemies?

It's easy to fall into the trap of taking hatred as nourishment. Just watch a hateful person sometime (or yourself when you are wrapped up in hate). Hatred is the soul's junk food, and once you eat one morsel, you can't stop. It's habit forming, and it robs the soul of peace. We all have to acquire a taste for forgiveness, understanding, patience, and love.

෧෧

Love your enemies
and pray for those who persecute you.
MATTHEW 5:44

How do you deal with discord?

Conflict swirls around us. Sometimes important matters are at stake; other times, folks fight over trivialities. At home, at work, at church, among friends, conflict jangles our nerves and leadens our hearts. Regardless of the cause of discord, however, it arouses in us a destructive need—the need to win. We respond by fighting to resolve things in the way we think best, and this compels us to speak and act violently.

In the midst of tension and confrontation, we lose sight of our priorities. Our need to engage in the fight entraps us. What we forget is that our first job in life is to be children of a loving God. The question we should ask ourselves on life's battlefields is not "How can I win?" but "How can I be a child of God in this situation?"

@∕@

Looking at God instantly reduces our disposition to dissent from our brother.
RALPH WALDO EMERSON

Do you enjoy having power over people?

Like the love of hatred, the love of power is destructive. The more power we have, the more we want. The problem is, power is only a temporary illusion. When we take pleasure in controlling others, we are really crying out about the control we don't have: we want to command our mortality, make others love us, live in physical and emotional safety, and dictate everyone else's beliefs. To find peace, you must recognize that real power is impossible and that, strangely, the people who have the greatest amount of power over their lives are those who let go of the impulse to control and have faith in God.

@@

You shall have joy, or you shall have power, said God;
you shall not have both.
RALPH WALDO EMERSON

Are you able to say, "I was wrong"?

Knowing that you are right and feeling obligated to defend your positions are compulsions that create anxiety. If you gently accept the fact that you don't know everything and that you can be wrong as easily as somebody else, the weight of intellectual pride falls from your body. The peaceful person is unsure of many things.

☯

Let us be humble; let us think that the truth may not perhaps be entirely with us.
JAWAHARLAL NEHRU

Are you able to say,
"I was wrong,
and you were right"?

Saying "I was wrong" is an important step in moving toward inner peace, but there's often another clause that ought to go with it which can stick in our throats: "You were right." For some of us it's easy enough to admit that we are mistaken, but saying that someone else was smarter or more insightful makes the matter competitive.

Once we let go of the notion that life's a game to be won, then acknowledging our own shortcomings and others' strengths becomes easy. In the end, we actually turn threatening situations into opportunities to praise and encourage others.

✺

He who speaks without modesty
will find it difficult to make his words good.
CONFUCIUS

Are you looking out for number one?

For good or ill, capitalism is a system in which many must fail so that a few may succeed. For this reason, people learn to "look out for number one." "Someone has to be the winner and someone the loser," we think, "and I mean to be the winner." The problem with this philosophy is that people who are always looking out for themselves are profoundly alone.

◉◉

Live for another if you wish to live for yourself.
SENECA

Who's happy?

When I was in college, one of my friends was a recovering alcoholic who came from a very wealthy family. He once made a remark about happiness I'll never forget. I think I can quote him verbatim: "These people at these AA meetings are some of the happiest people I've ever met. They just stand up and speak from the heart. They might not live in the best houses or drive the best cars, but they seem really happy."

Years later, after my own life-changing struggles, I think I know what my friend meant. There's something about walking through fire and coming out alive that leads to happiness. Just look at folks who have been to hell and back, and you'll see. Some of them seem remarkably peaceful.

Have you been through fire? Are you going through fire now? Have you wondered if there's hope for happiness? Please trust me when I tell you there is. I pray you will walk with God and find your way there.

@@

When one door of happiness closes, another opens; but often we look so long at the closed door that we do not see the one which has been opened for us.
HELEN KELLER

Do you sometimes feel useless?

It's natural to get down sometimes and feel as though our lives are meaningless. Yet if we think of ourselves as living in large part to help one another, then as long as we're trying to do one small thing to make the world a better place, as long as we are always on the lookout for the chance to support and to love, then we're never useless. If you are sympathetic, understanding, encouraging, or honest as often as possible, then your existence has meaning.

ॐ

So long as we love we serve;
so long as we are loved by others,
I would almost say that we are indispensable;
and no man is useless while he has a friend.
ROBERT LOUIS STEVENSON

Do you feel guilty for simply being human?

I once saw a movie (a pretty crummy one actually) in which a monk, upon seeing a naked woman, ran to his cell, threw his ceramic washing basin on the floor, and stood barefoot on the broken pieces. He wanted to drive the thought of the woman from his mind.

I'm sure we can all recognize that the monk was simply being human when he was aroused. Still, it's easy to tell others that they are "only human," but much more difficult to accept our own thoughts when they disturb us.

For many reasons, we struggle to love ourselves, to forgive and accept ourselves. We look into our hearts and see wounds, fractures, perversions. At least that's what *we* see. I believe that God sees human beings longing for peace in a tough world.

Sometimes we do wrong, and we ought to be able to admit that. Much of the time when we're loathing ourselves, however, we're feeling desperate to reach joy and hating ourselves for being duped by the fantasies we thought would take us there.

◎◎

I hate and love.
You ask, perhaps, how can that be?
I know not, but I feel the agony.
CATULLUS

Whom or what do you serve?

The word *servant* has negative connotations. Most of us want to have servants, not be one. Yet in a larger sense, we are all servants of something—generally something we just can't say no to. What can't you say no to? If you find that what you fervently love is a *thing* you can hold on to or a *thing* that profits you, you may want to look for a new lover—one who will snuggle up to you at night or offer a listening ear in times of distress.

@@

No one can serve two masters,
for a slave will either hate the one
and love the other, or be devoted to the one
and despise the other.
You cannot serve God and wealth.
MATTHEW 6:24

Do you want to be loved?

Although we should try to love people unconditionally—as God loves us—we should not assume that others will love us unconditionally. If we want to be loved, we need to demonstrate our love for others. We need to be energetic and cheerful in helping and generous with our time. We need to serve.

@@

If you'd be loved, be worthy to be loved.
OVID

Are you a source of light and life to others?

My mother used to get angry with me when I would refuse to do my chores without a smile on my face. I could never understand why she cared whether I was happy to do things like take out the garbage or do the dishes. What did it matter to her as long as the work was done? Now that I'm a little older I see her point. Help offered begrudgingly is really no help at all. Help offered with warmth and good cheer, on the other hand, is a source of light and life to all concerned, especially to the helper, who is mysteriously nourished by serving others without hoping for anything in return.

෨෨

*Keep a green tree in your heart
and perhaps the singing bird will come.*
CHINESE PROVERB

Are you in pain and in need of healing?

This world works in ways that foils your expectations. Exercise, mentioned earlier in this book, is one example. You'd think that exercise would tire you out, but it actually brings about energy and a sense of well-being. The same is true with giving to others. You'd think that giving to others would deplete your resources, but it restores them. Do you need healing in your life? Reach out to heal others.

✿✿

Giving to others heals me,
as the Indians healed themselves with herbs.
They did not understand what the herbs did,
how they operated, they only knew their healing
powers. So with me. I do not want to know what there
is about the process of giving that heals me. It is my
herb. I must not try to pick it apart. Just use it and
know what it does and be grateful.
CATHERINE DENEUVE

Do you get angry with God?

If you were raised and conditioned as I have been, you'd be reluctant, in a moment of great anger, to climb to a mountaintop and curse God. Why? Because you'd half expect a bolt of lightning to sizzle through your head.

But let's take a look at the world for a minute. Life can be viewed as confusing, violent, and disappointing. Thousands of religions tell us what to believe; people kill one another senselessly; and what we personally want the most, control, we are endlessly denied.

I probably sound silly, but I have to ask, what kind of God wouldn't understand that life is pretty tough on this planet and people are angry about it? Heck, lots of people I know can accept the anger of others; I have to believe that God's patience and wisdom are more abundant and generous than ours. I say, if you're mad at God, be mad. God can take it; besides, you may need to go through that anger to get to a better place.

⊙∕⊘

There lives more faith in honest doubt
Believe me, than in half the creeds.
ALFRED, LORD TENNYSON

Are you able to accept others
for who they are?

At the end of most episodes of *Mister Rogers' Neighborhood,* Fred Rogers says, "People can like you exactly as you are." For adults who are looking to put peace into their lives, Rogers has an important message. People *can* like us as we are, but we are also obligated to accept our loved ones in the same fashion, warts and all. Once you give up trying to change people, the burden of responsibility for others falls from you. You simply love others with no hope or expectation that they will ever change.

☙☙

Before we blame,
we should first see if we can't excuse.
G. C. LICHTENBERG

Do you try to see the best in others?

In the 1990s we live in a no-fault society: somebody is always to blame when something goes wrong, but that "somebody" is never "me." How much simpler the world would be if we would deal with the situation at hand rather than trying to punish those we hold responsible. How much more gratifying our relationships would be if we always tried to celebrate the best in one another.

❦

Let us no more contend, nor blame
Each other, blam'd enough elsewhere, but strive
In offices of love, how we may lighten
Each other's burden, in our share of woe.
JOHN MILTON

Do you compare yourself to others?

When we compare ourselves to others, we are usually either patting ourselves on the back or beating ourselves up. Only occasionally do we use comparisons legitimately (to acknowledge, for example, that others have the same problems and shortcomings we do and that we are not alone). Any time that you compare yourself with somebody else and feel proud or discouraged as a result, the comparison is probably invalid.

☯

Be aware that a halo has to fall
only a few inches to be a noose.
DAN MCKINNON

Do you have pet peeves?

Some people get so wrapped up in agonizing over pet peeves that they can spend hours feeling eaten up inside and sputtering like Yosemite Sam with his butt on fire. If you're like this, cut it out. Not a moment's peace should be sacrificed because a friend is always five minutes late or because a husband or wife hangs the toilet paper rolling the wrong way off the dispenser.

◎◎

One resolution I have made,
and try always to keep, is this:
To rise above little things.
JOHN BURROUGHS

Are you your own worst enemy?

As a teacher I have often seen students, particularly middle-aged students coming to college after many years out of the classroom, do well on writing assignments they never thought they could complete. They forget their wealth of life experience, which provides skills they aren't aware of. In the end, the biggest obstacle to their success is overcoming self-doubt. Never let a lack of confidence undermine your courage and resolve.

@@

What other dungeon is so dark as one's own heart!
What jailer so inexorable as one's self!
NATHANIEL HAWTHORNE

Do you put yourself down?

If you keep repeating something often enough, you begin to believe it. Unfortunately what you repeat sometimes minimizes your achievements and strengths. The next time somebody pays you a compliment, say thank you. Don't say, "Aw, shucks, anyone could've done it."

၆၅

Do not make yourself low;
people will tread on your head.
YIDDISH PROVERB

Do you respect yourself?

To find spiritual peace, we have to give ourselves abundantly to those around us—not out of obligation, but out of genuine love and kindness. We must act in a way that encourages us to be what we want to be; however, giving of ourselves doesn't mean we should neglect our own needs. Doing so shows a lack of self-respect. It's important to remember in the midst of generosity that if we aren't also respectful of our own needs, we'll have nothing to give to others.

@@

*If you want to be respected by others
the great thing is to respect yourself.
Only by that, only by self-respect will you
compel others to respect you.*
FYODOR DOSTOEVSKY

Do you know when to save yourself?

I believe that the road to peace calls us to give until it hurts. However, there are moments when continuing to give only destroys ourselves and accomplishes nothing. At such times, the ability to distance ourselves emotionally from turmoil can be life saving. It is possible to be a person of love and conviction and still lose battles of consequence. The key is never allowing detachment for survival's sake to slip into complete indifference.

๑๑

If you are losing a tug-of-war with a tiger,
give him the rope before he gets to your arm.
MAX GUNTHER

Do you know when to hit the Bozo Switch?

There are moments, particularly in work settings, when we encounter situations that are stupid, plain and simple. The outcomes are meaningless, the processes needlessly complicated, the energy devoted to the task ill spent. In such situations, we tend to get angry, even though we often have no choice but to carry on as if our actions were important.

At times like this, a friend of mine hits what he calls the Bozo Switch. He says to himself, "What I'm being asked to do is dumb, and I can't get out of it. I'm hitting the Bozo Switch. I will acknowledge the silliness of this business and refuse to waste my energy getting frustrated." In so doing, he gives Bozo situations only what they deserve.

☯

Those who realize their folly are not true fools.
CHUANG-TZU

Do you fight one battle at a time?

I hate to use warfare terminology, but let's face it, sometimes life can feel like a battle. The more time we spend in prayer and meditation, the more we can see ways we'd like to grow, wounds we'd like to heal, skills we'd like to hone, flames of old anger we'd like to douse.

As we hunger for peace, it's tempting to rush the process of growth and healing, but we need to be patient. Let's say you're hoping to become better at managing your time while dealing with the pain of a broken relationship. At such moments, it's good to pause and say, "One battle at a time." Let me get over this loss, then I'll worry about not being so harried all the time.

Of course, the risk in this philosophy is that some necessary battles never get fought. Maybe so. I suspect we're all going to our graves with more than a few items on our "to do" list. Perhaps this is a reality we just have to live with.

@@

There is time enough for everything
in the course of the day if you did but one thing
at once; but there is not time enough
in the year if you will do two things at a time.
LORD CHESTERFIELD

Do you own the world?

Sometimes our desire for control, even over small matters, can shake us to pieces. Not long ago, a friend told me about listening to a person give a presentation at a conference. It was clear, she said, that the presenter was very nervous, almost becoming unglued. My friend's own heart rate shot up, and her hands trembled.

I've found myself in that position many times; and I believe it's a result of trying to own the world. That is, we want so badly to control events that, emotionally and physically, we assume close to full responsibility for them. So we sweat along with the nervous speaker, eager to bring order to the chaos of a tense situation. Obviously, it's good to sympathize with a person who's suffering, but nobody benefits when we pester our minds and bodies with solidarity run amok.

Breathe deeply, love those who are having trouble, but let go of the fantasy that you must solve the problem at hand.

@@

Our duty is to be useful,
not according to our desires,
but according to our powers.
HENRY F. AMIEL

Do you get defensive in the face of criticism?

When somebody unfairly attacks us, our instinct is to strike back; however, the surest way to validate criticism is to become angry and defend oneself. The more we protest, the more guilty we sound—and, perhaps, the more we secretly suspect that the criticism is true. If somebody tries to make you feel inferior, don't get into an argument. If the statement against you is wrong, let it "twist in the wind." If it's true, be thankful that you have learned something about yourself.

๑๑

No one can make you feel inferior
without your consent.
ELEANOR ROOSEVELT

Is it possible that your weaknesses are really strengths?

One of the beauties and attractions of the cosmic dance is that we don't know all the answers to life's big questions. In fact, most of the time we don't even ask the right questions. Nevertheless, we slog ahead, assuming that eventually our own powers and intelligence will straighten out the world's problems. Ha! Most of us can't even straighten out our own lives alone. That's why we need to open ourselves to God's love and wisdom. Openness to God can show us that what we might view as a weakness is really a strength and vice versa. For example, let's say you're not a very snappy dresser and most of your clothes are pretty drab. You might think of this as a weakness, but the fact that your time and money are not tied up with fashion is an advantage in the search for spiritual peace. Not worrying about clothing creates emotional space for more worthwhile thinking that needs to be done in a full, rich life.

꩜

Do not deceive yourselves.
If you think that you are wise in this age,
you should become fools so that you may become wise.
For the wisdom of this world is foolishness with God.
1 CORINTHIANS 3:18–19

Are you honest with yourself?

"Be honest with yourself." It sounds easy enough, but it's tough to do. I suspect that the more honest we are with ourselves, the less certain we are about our self-diagnoses. Lots of times we just don't know what makes us the people we are or what motivates our actions. The key is to seek the truth about ourselves, to acknowledge uncertainty, and to cultivate an awareness of self-deception.

@@

Whatever games are played with us,
we must play no games with ourselves,
but deal in our privacy with the last honesty and truth.
RALPH WALDO EMERSON

Are you willing to share?

Think of how many lives have been lost in wars caused by nations that were unwilling to share wealth and resources; how many lives have been lost in famines caused by the world's failure to share food; how many marriages have been broken by the failure to share affection and time; how many friendships have been dissolved by the failure to share honesty and control.

෴

*There is enough in the world
for everyone to have plenty to live on
happily and to be at peace with his neighbors.*
HARRY S. TRUMAN

Is your soul singing?

As you travel the peace journey, you might find that what brings you pleasure changes. Maybe accumulating new possessions will make you content for a while, but when you spend enough time opening your heart to the Divine, you can feel your soul rejoicing in things you blew off before. A teenager with spiked florescent hair sings to an infant, and your soul sings. You look at the black limbs of a tree longing for the gray sky, and your soul sings. A muddy beagle jumps up on your lap and licks your chin, and your soul sings.

This soul singing is a gift from God, born of sitting in silence and allowing ourselves to be liberated by the potential for joy in these days we rush through, in this earth that spins beneath our feet.

@@

A happiness that is sought for ourselves alone
can never be found: for a happiness
that is diminished by not being shared
is not big enough to make us happy.
THOMAS MERTON

Are you strong enough to wage peace?

If somebody smaller and weaker than you punches you in the nose, what takes more strength, to punch back or to walk away? We often call the person left standing at the end of a fight the stronger of the two combatants. Yet the strongest person of all is the person who refuses to engage in violence and who realizes that violent people demonstrate intense self-hatred through their actions, which are best countered with acts of love. Mahatma Gandhi illustrated this point when a man jumped out of a crowd and began to strangle him. Gandhi responded by embracing the man, who fell weeping at Gandhi's feet.

@@

Courage is the price that life exacts for granting peace.
AMELIA EARHART PUTNAM

Do others have to suffer so you can succeed?

This is a dangerous question, for Western culture is built upon the notion that somebody must be number one; however, there's a big difference between trying to make a place for yourself in the marketplace and building an empire on broken people. Although success built on the suffering of others is rewarded materially in our culture, such success is a roadblock to spiritual peace. If you take pleasure in anybody's fall, you have violence in your heart.

๑๑

Do not hold the delusion that your advancement is accomplished by crushing others.
MARCUS TULLIUS CICERO

What's more important, rights or responsibilities?

One reason we have conflicts over social issues in our culture is that we favor rights over responsibilities. Think of two of the hottest debates in the United States at the end of the twentieth century: abortion and gun control. Both sides of the debate focus on what people should or should not be *allowed* to do, not on what they *should* do. In a rights-oriented society, the winners will be the ones who can beat up the other side. It's that simple.

❀

Do not expect justice where might is right.
PHAEDRUS

Do you worship in community?

I go to church every Sunday and am devout in doing so; nevertheless, I respect that this is not everybody's choice. For me, going to church is an opportunity to come together with others of roughly like mind for the purpose of joy.

It's important to get out on the dance floor of hope and acceptance, to lower your mask and let others see the God in your face, to affirm this good world in a song of the voice or heart.

How you worship in community is less important than that you do so. The point is that you celebrate your peace journey with others.

∞

It is Sunday, mid-morning—Sunday in the living room,
Sunday in the kitchen, Sunday in the woodshed,
Sunday down the road in the village:
I hear the bells, calling me to share God's grace.
E. B. WHITE

Are you building a peace community?

Our peace journeys can be intensely private and, therefore, difficult to share with others. We can't help but think that our family, friends, and colleagues will think we're spacey, out there, winged out, loopy.

Yet the peace journey, at least as this book presents it, is actually pretty sensible. We devote much time to learning—learning to accept reality and learning to look within ourselves and to our God for ways to cope with life. For this reason, we should be looking to teach others what we know. I'm not suggesting that we should be meddling know-it-alls, but we should acknowledge the power of spiritual peace and try to build communities of like-minded people who can nourish and comfort one another. I can't tell you the number of times my colleagues and I have been present to one another and have said words of healing and encouragement that have saved days from fatigue and despair. If you don't have a supportive community now, begin building one today. The benefits of sharing are incalculable.

☙

To teach is to learn twice over.
JOSEPH JOUBERT

Do you love peace?

A reasonable person's response to this question might be, "Sure, I love peace, but sometimes fighting is inevitable." I wonder, though, whether we "fight" as hard to prevent violence as we "fight" when the shooting begins.

When faced with problems, we often look to ourselves for peaceful solutions when we should look to God. We can't wage peace on earth alone. We have to open ourselves to God's inspiration to find healing in our relationships and among nations.

⚙⚙

O God of many names
Lover of all nations
We pray for peace
in our hearts
in our homes
in our nations
in our world
The peace of your will
The peace of our need.
GEORGE APPLETON

Do you demand too much of the earth?

As you grow toward spiritual peace, your field of vision expands. You notice things that slipped by you before. For example, as you think more and more about sharing, you begin to comprehend just how much there is to share—of yourself, your resources, and the resources around you. Eventually you wonder, driving by a landscape ravaged by strip mining, what you can do to conserve, to control your appetite for the world's gifts. What can you do? Begin with yourself.

@/@

Do not require too much of the universe;
there are other demands made upon it
which may conflict with yours.
You are part of a whole, and every other part
will expect you to remember it.
Ask too much and it shall not be given you;
knock too loudly and it shall not be opened unto you;
seek impatiently and you shall not find.

WILL DURANT

144

What can you do
to conserve resources **today?**

Why should a question like this appear in a book on spiritual peace? Because using our planet's (or perhaps the planet owns us?) gifts is another form of love and kindness, both of which are music in the cosmic dance. Besides, it's more fun to dance in tall grass than on a landfill. Today, turn off your water while you shave and brush your teeth, or walk to the corner store for your gallon of milk and carry with you a cloth bag.

◎◉

*Do not let spacious plans for a new world
divert your energies from saving what is left of the old.*
SIR WINSTON CHURCHILL

Can you give away what you love most?

You're eating a submarine sandwich. You're about six bites in and heading for the best part, where the salami, ham, and pepperoni are the thickest, the tomatoes and lettuce glistening in Italian dressing, the bread soft and warm. You paid five bucks for the whole sub, but four of them were for the best few bites. These bites are why you drove in the rain to the pizza shop, why you got soaked stepping in a puddle in the parking lot.

Here's the big moment. Then you look to the other side of the room and see a person you love. You forgot how much you love this person, how sitting in the same room and watching television with this person brings you joy. That person looks up and smiles, unaware that you're thinking of how blessed you are.

You stand up, take the sub over to your loved one and say, "Do you want a bite? It's really good." Your loved one takes a bite and smiles. Then you offer another. Then you sit back down. This is the best sub you've ever had.

@@

. . . it is in giving that we receive.
SAINT FRANCIS OF ASSISI

*Do you perform **secret** acts of kindness?*

One of the expressions of the day is "Commit random acts of kindness and senseless acts of beauty." I would also add that, in general, such acts should be secret. Of course, there's no need to hide or lie about what good we've done, but the purpose of a benevolent act is not to tell others so that they can congratulate us, at which point we move toward vanity.

Kind acts are food for our spirits. Just as you don't tell friends everything you eat in the course of a day, you don't need to mention all the elements of your spiritual nourishment.

֎

*Bounty always receives part of its value
from the manner in which it is bestowed.*
SAMUEL JOHNSON

How do you know you've done good?

A friend of mine, Erin, who is a chaplain at a university in Canada, called the other night and told a story about her hiring. During the interview process, it became clear to her that one of the women on the committee did not want the chaplaincy filled (for whatever reason), and she communicated with Erin only out of necessity. Over a couple of years, however, Erin continued to be herself, kind and gentle, and she became quite good friends with the woman. Not long ago, the woman stopped by Erin's office and said, "Sometimes I think God brought you here just to be my friend."

We can never tell what good will come of our trying to do what's good in the face of resistance. In the end, we behave as we believe we ought to and have faith that God will cultivate the blossoming.

🌀

Patience, and the mulberry leaf
becomes a silk gown.
CHINESE PROVERB

Do you look for opportunities to share?

We tend to see our money and possessions as things to preserve, and to the extent that saving helps us give to others and to ourselves wisely, then saving is good. I suspect that most often, however, we give in to our hoarding instinct. Being frugal is okay, but too much money and too many possessions eventually become a weight on the spirit.

☙❧

. . . they are so artless and so free with all they possess,
that no one would believe it without having seen it.
Of anything they have, if you ask them for it,
they never say no. Rather they invite the person
to share it, and show as much love
as if they were giving their hearts.
CHRISTOPHER COLUMBUS
ABOUT NATIVE AMERICANS

Do you always pick the parking place closest to the store?

Fred, a friend from church, always parks his truck on the street on Sunday mornings, even though there are usually spots available in the lot. One time I asked him why, and he said, "Other people need the spots closest to the church more than I do."

When I thought about it, I realized Fred was right. Our congregation includes lots of senior citizens and families with infants, and those who can walk without trouble ought to.

Can you imagine what this world would be like if in small matters we all looked for ways to be considerate. There wouldn't be enough space on the planet's surface to hold all the kindness.

@@

No act of kindness, no matter how small, is ever wasted.
AESOP

Should you be using the parking place farthest from the store?

Busy people struggle to find time to exercise, yet there are dozens of ways to make exercise your *modus operandi*. Taking the stairs instead of the elevator, reaching for the ceiling when you stand up from working, and parking some distance from your destination are all ways of sneaking exercise into a busy schedule. And any form of exercise makes you feel cleansed and energetic.

◎◎

Health is infinite and expansive in mode,
and reaches out to be filled with the fullness
of the world; wheras disease is finite and reductive
in mode, and endeavors to reduce the world to itself.
OLIVER SACKS

Do you have money in your heart?

If you live with money in your heart, then once you've gathered enough to satisfy your material wants, you'll find a vast emptiness before you. You'll have a nice home, nice cars, fine clothes, fine dining, fine everything. Then what?

◎◎

A wise man should have money in his head,
but not in his heart.
JONATHAN SWIFT

Can you give before you take?

I once watched a television report of a remarkable family. With an annual income of $30,000 or $40,000, they had managed over not many years to put away about $250,000. They went to great lengths to save money and figured that within another ten years the mother and father could retire and live on the interest of their savings.

This family had a lot to teach people about managing money, but one thing the father said troubled me: "Always pay yourself first." In other words, the first check you write when you get paid should be to your own savings account.

I suppose many financial planners agree with this, but I don't. For the sake of spiritual peace, the first check should be written to help others, and the amount should be substantial. Of course, the magic number for churches is 10 percent, the tithe. To me, the percentage is less important than the spirit in which the money is given. Even if the amount is small, it should be given lovingly and first, before bills are paid.

◎◎

It is not enough to do good;
one must do it in the right way.
JOHN MORLEY

Do you like to try new things?

At the risk of engaging in the "either/or" fallacy, I would argue that most people fall into one of two categories: those who like to try new things and those who do not. The explorers probably find peace more easily than those who are set in their ways because the explorers are adaptable. They figure out something tasty to have for breakfast when they run out of their favorite cereal; in fact, explorers look forward to an empty cereal box, which means that they get to try something else.

@@

Observe always that everything is the result of change, and get used to thinking that there is nothing Nature loves so well as to change existing forms and make new ones like them.
MARCUS AURELIUS

Do you love having your ideas challenged?

Many of us seeking spiritual peace love to control matters in our lives, and nothing is so disturbing as having to adjust our thinking. We like things the way they are! Unfortunately, life keeps shaking the ground we think is firm. As we grow older, the philosophies we live by get altered and softened by experience; fighting this evolution makes us disappointed and disillusioned. For example, the person who believes that the function of prayer is to ask God for all manner of things will surely grow haggard defending this belief. On the other hand, the person who allows her or his definition of prayer to evolve may find the result to be a richer communion with God. In the end, we can choose whether to take delight in or to battle with our changing ideas. Best to acquire a love for dancing as the ground shakes rather than trying to stand still and shattering to pieces.

❧❧

As long as you live, keep learning how to live.
SENECA

Do you see failure as an opportunity to learn?

Although grieving over failure and loss is necessary, we do an injustice to ourselves and our potential when we see *only* the negative side of pain. If each of us has redeeming qualities, they are born as much from our sorrows as from our joys. Patience is often the result of many agonizing vigils, compassion the blossom of much suffering. Look for the lessons in all situations.

◎◎

It is not always possible to know what one has learned,
or when the dawning will arrive. You will continue
to shift, sift, to shake out and to double back.
The synthesis that finally occurs can be in the most
unexpected place and the most unexpected time.
My charge . . . is to be alert to the dawnings.
VIRGINIA B. SMITH

Do you build upon the past?

When the past is painful, our instinct is to leave it behind entirely. We suppose that, by removing as many remnants of the past as possible from our lives, we can end our suffering. Only the most violent and terrorized history, however, has no redeeming qualities.

When it comes to our past, we are permitted to be complex, to at once mourn what's negative and to celebrate and build upon what's positive. For example, a friend of mine who was sexually abused by his father often talks about how much his father taught him about hard work and loyalty. Sounds strange, I know, but it's healthy to sift through the ashes of long ago and find things to be cleaned up, salvaged, redeemed.

@@

We may strive, with good reason, to escape it [the past], or to escape what is bad in it, but we will escape it only by adding something better to it.
WENDELL BERRY

Are you afraid to fail?

If you've been watching sporting events on television over the past few years, you may have noticed that silver and bronze medalists are considered failures. If an athlete doesn't win the gold, then reporters interview her or him as if second or third place is like a death in the family. No wonder many people are afraid to attempt new things. Our response to the possibility of falling on our faces ought to be, "So what? At least i'm living and trying and having a ball!"

@@

Make voyages!—Attempt them!—
there's nothing else . . .
TENNESSEE WILLIAMS

Do you make life interesting?

I suppose we all become bored from time to time, but we can learn to make the smallest things in life wonderfully interesting with a little creativity and energy. Here's an example from my own bag of tricks (you're going to think I'm a weirdo, but here goes): When I'm home during the day, I always peek out the window before I check the mail. I look for any clues outside that will tell me whether the mail's arrived before I open the box. Mail sticking out is a sure sign, but there are other more subtle ways of predicting. From my window, I can see four houses across the street. If none of the boxes has mail sticking out, I'm betting the mail hasn't come yet. If there's snow on the ground, I can tell by the arrangement of footprints on the porch whether we've gotten mail.

I know this sounds silly, but just as the everyday can be sacred, so too can it be engaging.

☺☺

You see but you do not observe.
SHERLOCK HOLMES
TO DR. WATSON / ARTHUR CONAN DOYLE

Do you worship energy?

In writing this book I have sought to welcome various pathways to peace, for I realize that folks have many different ways of getting there. Still, I can't help but view constant motion as an obstacle to peace. To be fair, I'd say the same thing about bone idleness.

The problem is, busyness is revered in our culture. I would argue, however, that a person who feels intensely uncomfortable at 11 P.M., when the day's labor is hushed, is running from something. Energy is a great thing, but not always so noble as we pretend. Sometimes it's a substitute for the wailing we might do when we sit still long enough to greet despair.

೧೦

The worshipper of energy is too physically energetic to see that he cannot explore certain higher fields until he is still.
CLARENCE DAY

Can you love the friend
and hate her or his actions?

In asking this question, I have changed the phrasing of an expression often heard among Lutherans: "Hate the sin; love the sinner." I write almost nothing about "sin" in this book because in using this term, we focus too much on specific actions and too little on understanding what sin really is (and here, of course, I can only offer my own definition). To me, sin is looking for God where God is not, searching for peace where peace is not, and lashing out in one way or another when we don't find what we're looking for.

When we recognize sin as an attempt to find happiness that comes up empty, we can see universal hunger for God in all our brothers and sisters and aspire to offer them *agape*—unconditional, spotless, Godlike love.

@@

Your friend is the man who knows all about you,
and still likes you.
ELBERT HUBBARD

Can you forgive people
who have caused you pain?

Grudges large and small are as much a physical as a mental phenomenon. Sure, hatred clouds the mind and inhibits concentration, but it also acts as a bitter weight on the body. If you want to dance the light dance of peace, you need to let go of ill will. When you don't forgive, you allow the people who have hurt you to continue hurting you. Of course, you must work through anger and resentment, but at the end of that process must come love and mercy.

⚭⚭

We must develop and maintain the capacity to forgive.
He who is devoid of the power to forgive is devoid of the
power to love. There is some good in the worst of us
and some evil in the best of us. When we discover this,
we are less prone to hate our enemies.

DR. MARTIN LUTHER KING JR.

Can you forgive yourself
for the pain you have caused others?

Perhaps the hardest person to forgive for inflicting pain is yourself. In a strange way, we are as attracted to guilt as we are to hatred, and like hatred, guilt is lead on the body and spirit. After we have asked for forgiveness from others and from God and have tried to make amends, then we need to take the final step and grant ourselves forgiveness. (By the way, the Twelve Steps of recovery embraced by Alcoholics Anonymous and other such organizations suggests making substantial amends for wrongs committed.)

@@

Do as the heavens have done, forget your evil,
With them forgive yourself.
WILLIAM SHAKESPEARE

Do you want forgiveness from God and others?

In the Bible one requirement for forgiveness is repeated time and again, and it's appropriate here as well: if you want other people and God to forgive you, you must forgive others. No options here. Forgiveness doesn't happen all at once, but it must be an assumed eventuality.

◉◉

Whenever you stand praying, forgive,
if you have anything against anyone;
so that your Father in heaven may also
forgive you your trespasses.
MARK 11:25

What is forgiveness?

Not long ago I discovered that a man in my neighborhood was sexually abusing children. When he confessed to the abuse, he also asked the community for forgiveness. For the first time in my life, I found that I was unable to forgive—at least in the way I had always defined forgiving.

Like most other people, I've spent my whole life assuming that forgiving people means letting them off the hook. In this case, the number one priority was that kids be protected; to forgive would have endangered kids—no deal. Fortunately, my pastor, Cheryl, offered an important insight: I could forgive and still expect the abuser to realize the consequences of his actions. I can work to remove hatred from myself, to wish the abuser no ill, to commend him to God's care, but forgiveness does not alter the fact that his actions have consequences.

◎∾

In nature there are neither rewards nor punishments—
there are consequences.
ROBERT GREEN INGERSOLL

Can you come clean?

Often when we hear the word *forgiveness,* we think of being absolved from something we did in the past. Rarely do we think of cleansing the future, which is really the most powerful aspect of confession and forgiveness. I once heard a pastor tell a story about a couple he had counseled prior to their marriage. Both the man and the woman had had numerous sexual partners, about forty between the two of them, and in the course of the discussions the issue of trust came up. All three of them wondered how there could be trust in this marriage. The pastor suggested that they confess their previous behavior to one another and ask for forgiveness as a first step toward this trust. When they did this, all three of them wept, feeling as they did the power of God to heal and restore integrity.

The power of "coming clean" for this couple wasn't so much that it negated all they had done, but that it empowered them to trust one another and live up to their promise of faithfulness.

๏๏

Confession of our faults is the next thing to innocence.
PUBLILIUS SYRUS

Do you feel an emptiness that can't be filled?

One reason you're reading this book right now is that you've answered yes to the above question. I think we all walk around at least some of the time with the feeling that we're missing something, that there ought to be something more to life, that we're hungry but we don't know what we're hungry for. Life contains a lot of longing, and we need to look to our spiritual journeys for answers and new questions, not to material things. We also need to know that longing never goes away completely.

ᐩᐩ

The mass of men lead lives of quiet desperation.
HENRY DAVID THOREAU

Are you disillusioned?

In my experience, most disillusionment comes from unfulfilled expectations. We try to help out a friend, for example, and receive no gratitude in return. Or we watch a good person die young and painfully.

When we focus on results, disappointment is inevitable; however, when we concentrate on processes, we are more able to recognize the goodness of life. In letting our assistance to our friend be its own reward, we forget to listen for a "thank you." We feel it in the air. In celebrating life, any life, we see the privilege of being on this earth, even for a short time.

I'm not trying to paint an unreasonably rosy picture here. There is indeed cause for disillusionment in the world—but far less than we seem willing to accept.

֍֎

The hours we pass with happy prospects in view
are more pleasing than those crowned with fruition.
OLIVER GOLDSMITH

Are you disappointed when you finally get things you've been waiting for?

By now you know that this book challenges materialistic thinking. Clearly the reason that we're so often disappointed when our wishes are at last granted is that we expect specific things (e.g., a remodeled kitchen, a BMW, even a new friend) to fill that empty space. Sometimes we get lucky and a possession or a change in circumstances will fill our souls a bit, but in the long run the dance we want to attend is cosmic, not earthly.

@/@

Learn to level down your desires
rather than level up your means.
GREEK PROVERB

Do you identify your experiences as "good" or "bad"?

Here's an interesting story from Bill Moyers's television program *The Wisdom of Faith,* which I will paraphrase: a man went out to his pasture one day and discovered that his horse was gone. A friend said to him, "How terrible! You must be sad."

The man replied, "Who can say what is good or bad?"

The next day his horse returned, followed by a dozen wild horses. His friend said, "What luck! You must be happy."

The man said, "Who can say what is good or bad?"

The next day, while trying to break one of the wild horses, his son fell off and broke his leg.

The man's friend said, "What bad luck."

You know what the man said. The next day military officials stopped to find all young, able-bodied men to fight in a pending war. His son couldn't fight on one good leg and was not drafted.

Who *can* say what is good or bad?

@@

I feel my fate in what I cannot fear.
I learn by going where I have to go.
THEODORE ROETHKE

Is unfulfilled longing good?

Some intellectuals would have us believe that life is all *process* and that *product* is inconsequential. Mainstream society, on the other hand, reinforces the idea that product is all and that process is secondary (the end justifies the means). I would argue that life is both, with most of our time devoted to process. It's healthy to remember this fact: our days are given primarily to reaching for things, even spiritual peace, and that once we grab hold of one thing, we sit back for a moment or two, then find something else to reach for. This being the case, we'd better start regarding longing and reaching as positives.

ᥐᥐ

Life is a progress from want to want,
not from enjoyment to enjoyment.
SAMUEL JOHNSON

Are you getting buried by your ancestors?

I don't pretend to possess the experience of many years, but the older I get, the more I see people of my generation (late baby boomers) getting crushed by the expectations of our parents' generation. I'm not sure what the statistics tell us, but I see the people around me breaking to pieces in an attempt to gain approval from elders.

I suspect each generation in some measure crushes the next, but the fact is, we don't need to lie still for it. I'm not suggesting angry rebellion against elders, but quiet reflection: To what extent are our actions controlled by our desire to please parents, grandparents, in-laws, other relatives, older friends? How much sorrow and disappointment are we feeling when we see ourselves fall short of their expectations? Are their expectations valid? healthy? reasonable? timeless?

We crave praise from elders. It tastes good, but we spend a king's ransom of spiritual peace purchasing it.

❧❧

The imitativeness of our early years makes us
acquire the passions of our parents,
even when these passions poison our lives.
STENDHAL [MARIE-HENRI BEYLE]

Are you still being your parents' child?

A friend of mine once said that no matter how old he gets, he always feels like a twelve-year-old when he's with his dad. Indeed, in the presence of the others, it's hard for parents to remember that their kids have grown up and hard for kids to *feel* as though they've grown up. It's good to have a mom and dad, to preserve some of the comfort of those bonds, but if we are to make a mature and courageous peace journey, we as children must encourage our parents to behave as friends who treat us with respect. Needless to say, we must also be friends to our adult children.

◎◎

If you want a baby, have a new one.
Don't baby the old one.
JESSAMYN WEST

Do you sometimes feel like a lazy slug?

If there's one problem with the spiritual journey, it's that a good bit of it is devoted to philosophizing. We learn to sit still and pray, to view the world in a positive fashion, to begin loving and forgiving, and then we can't seem to get our butts out of our chairs. As we contemplate ourselves and our world, we need to remember that there's no substitute for action; moreover, action often leads to insights that intellectualizing never provides.

@@

> *. . . all the beautiful sentiments in the world*
> *weigh less than a single lovely action.*
> JAMES RUSSELL LOWELL

Do you have trouble getting started?

As a teacher of writing, and as a writer myself, I hear the same valid complaint over and over: "I can't get started. Once I get started I'm okay." Isn't it this way with many tasks. Taking the first step, writing the first sentence, putting on the sweat suit, getting out the paint and brushes, washing the first dish—the hardest part is getting under way.

The key to putting things in motion is to focus on the first step, not on the ultimate goal. The latter is intimidating, big, insurmountable. The former is friendly, little, easy. For example, if you want to get physically fit, don't think about power walking and losing twenty pounds. Think about walking up and down your stairs two or three times today.

✪

Our main business is not to see what lies dimly
at a distance, but to do what lies clearly at hand.
THOMAS CARLYLE

*Do you avoid starting for fear
of not being able to finish?*

How many dreams have withered because dreamers don't know how to proceed, fear failure, can't see the destination hiding somewhere beyond layers of horizons? Particularly when dreams deserve to be realities, we ought to chase them—even when it makes little sense to do so—not because we'll succeed, but because the effort, the bravery, the foolishness are all food for our souls. Realizing the dream isn't the point. The dreamer's dancing is itself the destination.

◎◎

Begin to weave and God will give the thread.
GERMAN PROVERB

*Do you come up with lots of good reasons
not to do things that you know you ought to do?*

Of course you do. We all do. It's called rationalizing, and more than holding us back from growing, it insults our intelligence. We know, even as we're rationalizing, that we're full of baloney. In "The Woman at the Washington Zoo," Randall Jarrell writes of a person caught in stagnation. In desperation, the speaker of the poem says, "Oh bars of my body, open, open." If we want the "bars" of our bodies and souls to open, we need to act at that moment when we catch ourselves listing reasons for not doing what we need to do. Our growth depends on it.

☯☯

*And oftentimes excusing of a fault,
Doth make the fault the worse by the excuse.*
WILLIAM SHAKESPEARE

Do you appreciate all that you have?

If you find yourself living from paycheck to paycheck and feel sorry for yourself, just turn on the evening news. On practically any broadcast you can see children starving and people dodging gunfire. If you had enough money to buy this book, take a few moments and note the things you take for granted, things that millions don't have: a light to read by, a glass of clean water, a piece of bread, a bathroom, a blanket. Give thanks today.

◎◎

Be satisfied, and pleased with what thou art,
Act cheerfully, and well th' allotted part;
Enjoy the present hour, be thankful for the past,
And neither fear, nor wish, th' approaches of the last.
MARTIAL

*Do you appreciate all that you **do not** have?*

It's odd to think of giving thanks for what we don't have, but remember that with ownership comes responsibility. Let's say, for example, that you can finally afford that new dining room set you've been wanting for ten years. When it's in your dining room, you find, to your dismay, that you can't relax while eating because you're afraid your kids will gouge the table with a fork. Or you get nervous that your portly uncle will lean back on a chair and crack one of the legs. Ah, it's so pleasant to finally have that shiny, important table and chairs—not to mention the china cabinet with glass doors!

∽∾

*. . . I regard everything as loss
because of the surpassing value of knowing
Christ Jesus my Lord. For his sake I have suffered
the loss of all things, and I regard them as rubbish,
in order that I may gain Christ and be found in him. . . .*
PHILIPPIANS 3:7–9

Do you appreciate what does not belong to you?

If you stop and think about it, ownership doesn't matter much. If you love the line of poplar trees bordering your neighbor's yard, the fact that the trees do not belong to you should have no effect on your enjoying them. Many things of beauty are beyond ownership—birds, laughter, the sound of children singing.

◎◎

Touch the earth, love the earth, honour the earth,
her plains, her valleys, her hills, and her seas;
rest your spirit in her solitary places.
HENRY BESTON

How will you feel about today's crisis
five years from now?

One technique I use when I feel overwhelmed by one problem or another is to ask myself how I'll feel about the situation in five years. A good example of this occurred when I was in graduate school a little over ten years ago. I went through several days of stomach-strangling agony over something the details of which I swear I can't remember anymore. I think it was over a part-time teaching job I was hoping to get—maybe. The point is, the crisis that had my knees wobbling was pretty minor in the long run. I suspect much of our turmoil is caused by things we may not remember next month, let alone next year.

೦⁄೦

I've had lots of troubles in my life—
most of which never happened.
SATCHEL PAIGE

Is your peace journey
making you do weird stuff?

The peace journey can make you do things that you would have considered a little bizarre only a short time ago. For example, a few months ago I went to visit Edna Mae, a woman from my church who was in a nursing home. When I checked in at the reception desk, I was told that Edna Mae had suffered a stroke just the day before. I went to her room and found her sleeping, her jaw open and slack.

I decided not to awaken her. Instead, I looked around her room for a time, at old photographs of her and her late husband and of her children and grandchildren. Sitting in a chair by her bed, I recalled the times I visited her before and listened as she begged to go home. I just sat there for a while in the dim light, in the presence of her last days, and tried to be a silent friend for a few moments. Her dying was a good thing, an overdue passage into what I believe will be warmth, light, joy beyond telling.

Were it not for my own journey, I'd have just walked away.

☺☺

Peace is when time doesn't matter as it passes by.
MARIA SCHELL

Who are you?

About an hour before writing this, I listened to a talk by K. Leroy Irvis, a former state official in Pennsylvania who started the Act 101 Program, which provides benefits for educationally and economically disadvantaged college students in Pennsylvania. He told the story of the program's birth: One Sunday evening he was called into a meeting behind closed doors with other high-ranking officials to put together a state budget. The person running the meeting went around the table and asked each man (men only in those days) what he needed. Irvis hadn't known that he would be asked this question and had no time to plan his response. When it was his turn, he found himself saying, "I need five million for a program for disadvantaged college kids." Irvis's response came from who he was, the great accumulation of experiences, ideas, and emotions that defined him. You are at the middle of this book, and it seems like a good time to ask, "Who are you?" When you have to respond, no time for planning or posturing, may your name be Love.

@@

Philosophy forms us for ourselves, not for others;
to be, not to seem.
MICHEL DE MONTAIGNE

Whose are you?

Twice this book asks you the question, "Who are you?" It's good to put a lot of thought into answering this question, yet if you're like me, what you come up with is never quite whole or satisfying; in fact, we may never come to a conclusion. As a result, we might feel a lack of identity.

We don't have to feel this way, for the equally valid companion question to "Who are you?" is "Whose are you?" When you can say, "I belong to God," you answer, in a holistic way, the former question. Belonging to God means that you are, or are trying to be, the face of the loving Divine to those around you.

@

*God is the indwelling and not
the transient cause of all things.*
BARUCH SPINOZA

Are you sometimes unable to make people understand your peace journey?

I can't pretend to explain why, but some people will not understand your search for spiritual peace. Perhaps they have not suffered as you have. Perhaps they have an ability to overlook unhappiness, to muscle their way through fear and confusion.

I'm not this way, and I suspect if you're getting into this book, you're not either. What we all need to accept is that people have different ways of being happy, and some will never understand that your path includes seeking solitude, loving abundantly, giving foolishly. The danger is in thinking less of those who don't accept your route to peace. Don't do this. Accept people who can't accept you.

◎◎

No man can reveal to you aught but that which already lies half asleep in the dawning of your knowledge.
KAHLIL GIBRAN

Do you trust people?

No one can deny that people betray one another. The problem is, much of the time it is difficult if not impossible to anticipate betrayal. What's the solution? The peaceful person must be willing to trust people and be made the fool from time to time. Mistrusting people simply takes more energy than it's worth. Believe people unless they give you a reason not to, and know that sometimes you will be wrong.

◎◎

> *The most distrusting persons*
> *are often the greatest dupes.*
> PAUL DE GONDI

Can you submit to other wisdoms?

Although ego may yield some benefits, it generally gets in the way of spiritual peace because it makes us more comfortable about our own "wisdom" than we ought to be. People of light and life drift through our days and pass along to us healing messages which bounce off our stony heads because we've already got it all figured out.

When we are able to hear, we find solutions, comforts, startling pathways to joy that only others can lead us to. It's tempting to project our confidence and intelligence; yet we're strongest when we admit our limitations and open our spirits to the great cloud of other wisdoms we wander through each day.

@@

He who yields a prudent obedience,
exercises a partial control.
PUBLILIUS SYRUS

Can you assume the perspective
of a person with whom you disagree?

One of the best ways of resolving conflict is to take the place of the person with whom you disagree. If two people simply knock heads together, the result is usually two headaches, but if two people try to understand one another, conflict can lead to growth and healing.

೦೦

*You will learn more by agreeing in the main
with others and entering into their trains of thinking,
than by contradicting and urging them to extremities.*
WILLIAM HAZLITT

Can you give up self-interest?

Although few of us consider ourselves selfish, many of us act primarily out of self-interest. What we fail to realize is that often our own needs are best served by focusing on somebody else's needs. Let's say you have kids and they're especially grouchy one evening. Your reaction might be, "I'm tired and need rest, and they just won't cut me a break." If you continue thinking of your own needs, you'll be in conflict with your kids for the rest of the night, but if you focus on their needs for just half an hour, it's possible that they'll cheer up and you'll get some of the peace and quiet you need.

$\textmd{\textcircled{\small{∞}}}$

I have been a selfish being all my life,
in practice, though not in principle.
JANE AUSTIN

Are you willing to lose?

The person who wants to be at peace has to escape the black/white, right/wrong, either/or, love it or leave it, my way or no way sensibility. To find peace you have to be honest, and if you're honest you know that you're wrong a good bit of the time. Don't be afraid to let others know that you are willing to lose.

@⁄@

There is a time in life when you have to back off.
WALTER ANNENBERG

Echo question:
Are you getting to know your own body?

Just as our spirits shout to warn us of some deep un-happiness, our bodies also have their own ways of cry-ing: headaches, colds, intestinal brouhahas. Sometimes spirit and body bump into each other. We try to medi-tate, for example, and we can't because we've been ig-noring the signals our bodies have been sending us that we're stressed or unhappy.

It's time, therefore, to renew our awareness of what our bodies do to let us know we're suffering and don't realize it. It's also time to suggest again that tak-ing care of the body is a critical part of a spiritual dis-cipline. A fit body will let the spirit do its work and dance its dance.

@@

All the soarings of my mind begin in my blood.
RAINER MARIA RILKE

Are you falling in love with maxims?

A couple of people who have been kind enough to read over this book as I've been writing it have seemed particularly fond of the quotations at the end of each meditation. I like them, too. The only problem is that it's tempting to take them for more than they really are—an exquisite way of phrasing a general truth.

I'm ever mindful of our tendency toward absolutes. I don't suppose that one meditation in 366 is too much to devote to reminding all of us that we need to maintain balance. The quotes in this book are true most of the time, but just when you think you've got a good, hearty blanket statement on your hands, a sassy little objection pokes its head from under the covers.

☙

Few maxims are true in every respect.
LUC DU CLAPIERS DE
MARQUIS VAUVENARGUES

Must something be factual to be true?

I've recently read magazine articles and watched videos that examine the historical accuracy of Scripture. Here's some of what they come up with: Jesus was born in 4 B.C.; he started out as a disciple of John the Baptist, not the other way around; there's no evidence that Abraham of the Old Testament ever existed. There's more, but you get the idea.

I'm sure the same historical research has been done on the documents of many faiths, and the fear of believers is that taking away factual authenticity compromises the validity of the belief. For me, the wisdom revealed in the world's religions and spiritual practices don't hinge on whether concepts can be tied to verifiable events.

On this subject, Sister Rita, one of my prayer mentors, said, "I don't know whether some of the things in Scripture really happened, but I know they're true."

◎◎

To know, to get into the truth of anything,
is ever a mystic act, of which the best logics
can but babble on the surface.
THOMAS CARLYLE

Do you possess negative capability?

The term "negative capability," coined by the poet John Keats in the quotation below, means the capacity to exist comfortably in the absence of answers. Being able to rest in uncertainty is essential for peace. Without negative capability, we feel tension about and responsibility for stupid things. The question "What was Stonewall Jackson's real first name?" becomes monumentally important. If you don't know Jackson's first name, practice not worrying about finding out.

◎◎

At once it struck me, what quality went to form a Man of Achievement especially in literature & which Shakespeare possessed so enormously—I mean Negative Capability, *that is, when man is capable of being in uncertainties, Mysteries, doubts, without any irritable reaching after fact & reason.*
JOHN KEATS

Can you say, "I don't know"?

The manifestation of the absence of negative capability is the inability to say, "I don't know." Have you ever heard a person continue to guess and ponder until you're ready to scream (maybe you're one of those people). How much easier and stress free to say those words that expose us as imperfect and of average intelligence: "Ya got me."

@@

Be not proud because thou art learned,
but discourse with the ignorant man as with the sage.
PTAHHOTEP

Do you question questions?

When somebody asks us a question, we tend to assume that our reply should be in the form of an answer; however, some questions really deserve questions in return. For example, a parent might say to a college student who fails a class, "You're being lazy, aren't you? People who fail classes are either lazy or stupid, and I know you're not stupid." The student's impulse might be to launch a counterattack replete with a study schedule and tales of sleepless nights of cramming. After all of this, the parent might remain firm.

The student would be best off replying with a question: "Why do you assume that laziness or stupidity are the only reasons for getting an 'F'?" Many times each day, we get sucked into struggling against faulty or mean-spirited questions. In such cases, we need to address the *issue,* not necessarily the question. In doing so, we avoid getting into a silly wrestling match with an empty overcoat.

◎◎

There is no right answer to a wrong question.
AUTHOR UNKNOWN

Does peace contradict itself?

I have been working on this book for a few years now, and I rejoice in the blessings of my peace journey. As a poet and fiction writer, I've always carried with me the famous notion that writing should bring order to chaos and make some sense of the world.

I think at this point, however, it's important to acknowledge that no honest writer can or should sweep away the messiness and contradictions along the road toward peace. We're constantly learning new things, getting blind-sided by suffering, and stumbling into startling gifts. Something we're sure of one day is full of flaws the next.

We need to celebrate those moments when a bit of order shimmers in the chaos, but mostly we need to befriend the chaos and see our confusion as jitterbugs in the cosmic dance.

@

He who confronts the paradoxical exposes himself to reality.
FRIEDRICH DÜRRENMATT

Are you able to accept the inevitable?

We can't stand quitters. We applaud people who refuse to give up in the face of bad odds, yet sometimes the greatest demonstration of strength is surrendering. Accepting the inevitable doesn't mean that we give up trying, but that we relax and deal with all the possibilities. If one has a terminal illness, one needn't give up hope of a cure, but putting on blinders to the prospect of death is to deny reality and to rob oneself of the death experience. Being realistic, even if that means being scared and sad, takes strength and intelligence.

@@

*Let us try to see things as they are
and not wish to be wiser than God.*
GUSTAVE FLAUBERT

Do you recognize and deal with loss?

For many years, conventional wisdom told people to deal with loss by getting busy, by not sitting around and moping. Although there is some merit to this philosophy, grief must be experienced. Sometimes we're so busy that we feel the sadness and grief, but we don't identify it or connect it to a specific loss in our lives. If we don't try to make such connections, we float along on a sea of pain and never quite know why. Examining pain gives us the power to move beyond it.

✪

I have always believed that God never gives a cross to bear larger than we can carry.
ROSE KENNEDY

Can you say, "I'm afraid"?

When I was growing up, my family used the saying "keep a stiff upper lip" a lot. Though I still find myself controlled by and occasionally grateful for that philosophy, I now prefer openness and vulnerability. If you are afraid, then you don't need to pretend you're brave, and if you don't need to pretend, then you don't need to lie, and if you don't need to lie, then the door for peace is open. If you lie, the door for peace is shut.

◎◎

Fear not, provided you fear;
but if you fear not, then fear.
BLAISE PASCAL

Can you say, "I'm afraid, but I don't care"?

There is one beautiful thing about fear—it is in the mind. Fear is not a brick wall or a crippled limb. It is an attitude. However, fear becomes much more of a brick wall when you deny it than when you acknowledge it. When you say, "I'm afraid," you empower yourself to also say, "I'm going to work past my fear."

◎◎

It was a high counsel that I once heard
given to a young person,
"Always do what you are afraid to do."
RALPH WALDO EMERSON

During times of trouble,
do you feel particularly spiritual?

Although nobody likes to go through tough times, many of the peaceful people I know remark that they actually appreciate the heightened sense of the Divine presence they experience during their struggles. If I didn't think as they did, I'd probably accuse them of being masochistic. The fact is, the peace journey helps us to stop seeing our lives in terms of bad and good times; rather, regardless of our circumstances, we know that God is with us. Tough times, then, become a time to draw close to God.

@@

I have had prayers answered—most strangely so
sometimes—but I think our heavenly Father's
loving kindness has been even more evident
in what He has refused me.
LEWIS CARROLL

What is liberty?

What is liberty? (1) Doing what we really want to do, or (2) really wanting what we do. For those who are politically or personally oppressed, some taste of answer one has to come before answer two. But for those of us who enjoy the freedom to do pretty much as we please, liberty doesn't mean living in a hedonistic frenzy. It means being free of the lust that drags us around like fools, lies, and laughs in our faces. Liberty, then, isn't doing what we want, it's wanting what we do.

@@

What nature requires is obtainable,
and within easy reach.
It's for the superfluous we sweat.
SENECA

Do you burn bridges?

Most burned bridges are ignited by anger and rashness. We shouldn't burn bridges, not because we limit our options (though this isn't an invalid reason), but because in anger and haste we often do stupid violence and cause pain. So we keep bridges intact because a standing bridge means that we have striven for understanding and reconciliation.

@@

It is too rash, too unadvised, too sudden;
Too like the lightning, which doth cease to be
Ere one can say it lightens.
WILLIAM SHAKESPEARE

Do you use silence as a weapon?

What is violence? Some people who consider themselves pacifists seem very violent to me. Despite all of the publicity in recent years on psychological abuse, lots of very bright people fall into the trap of supposing that violence is always physical, loud, or in some way coercive. One of the most damaging instruments I have seen people use against one another, however, is silence. There is injury in forced isolation, in the deliberate withholding of communication.

People shut one another out and get shut out themselves on a daily basis, and to expect somebody to make a big deal out of these whitecaps in the flow of our daily interaction is probably silly. Still, the peaceful spirit should recognize invisible weapons and avoid using them.

෨෨

> *Violence is essentially wordless, and it can begin*
> *only where thought and rational communication*
> *have broken down.*
> THOMAS MERTON

Do you try to make people feel guilty?

Making others feel guilty is primarily a way of holding power over them. As usual, we want to have the upper hand in our relationships, and if we can dictate our loved one's emotions, then we rest secure. For example, if a loved one feels guilty for making us late for an appointment and we encourage that guilt, then he or she can't make us feel guilty. As long as we can claim to be in the right, we have won. But what is the prize? A loved one's suffering.

@@

Forgive, son; men are men, they needs must err.
EURIPIDES

Do you ask for the impossible?

During the past couple of years a handful of books and numerous magazine articles have been published on differences between the sexes. Many argue that we need to accept that men and women are different and stop torturing ourselves trying to be what we are not.

Such generalizing might be a comfort to some, might even provide useful, valid insights for certain men and women who are in conflict with one another; however, the peace journey demands that we categorize with care. In my experience, categorizing makes people feel inadequate as often as it unifies them.

The point is, we need to understand that some characteristics of people can change, and others may be permanent—part of the make-up. When we ask people to change what they are, we may be asking too much.

☙☙

Wood may remain ten years in the water,
but it will never become a crocodile.
CONGOLESE PROVERB

Can you find nonviolent ways to vent anger?

As we move along the peace journey, hopefully we gradually reduce violent emotions like hatred, anger, jealousy; however, all emotions must be experienced and processed, or they fester inside of us. I use running to process anger. Others use weight lifting, walking, swimming, singing or playing a musical instrument, sculpting, painting, biting pillows, and hollering in the woods. Whatever method we use to vent anger, the trick is to avoid making others suffer as we deal with our emotions.

☯☯

Violence can never bring an end to violence;
all it can do is provoke more violence.
MAHATMA GANDHI

Is anger your vice?

To tell the truth, anger can feel pretty good sometimes, especially when you let it out. I suspect if it were legal to run around naked and howl at the full moon, people would engage in the vice of anger less often. But since it's difficult to find an appropriate expression of our frustrations at living in a world we can't control, we often cultivate large disruptions and small annoyances into many gardens of anger. We swear at the slow driver in front of us, scream at our kids for forgetting to put their socks on, come positively unglued when we don't get the raise we think we deserve.

No doubt some anger is justified and worthy of acknowledging and processing, but when we seem to be ingesting anger, then healthy functioning turns to an invisible form of self-mutilation.

@@

Holding on to anger is like grasping a hot coal with the intent of throwing it at someone else—
you are the one who gets burned.
BUDDHA

Is there room for anger in your relationships?

People often judge the health of a relationship by the absence of disputes. If those in a relationship don't argue, the thinking goes, then things must be going well; not so. Enduring friendships and marriages are not built by trying to avoid fighting, but by trusting one another enough to let some anger and annoyance be okay. If you're mad at your friend, for example, it's much better to say, "I'm mad right now. Give me a little time to be mad and sort things out, and then we can talk." In the end, you'll have more honesty and less tension in your relationships if disagreements aren't viewed as threatening, but as natural and inevitable.

๑๏

It is better to talk it out in a forum
than to fight it out in an arena.
TOM LEHRER

Do you get angry with yourself?

Just as it's okay to get angry with people we love, it's also okay to get upset with ourselves. The key to dealing effectively with all anger is to see it for what it is (temporary, typical, a bit foolish) and to detach ourselves from it. When we're caught up in self-flagellation, it's good to step back and say, "What am I so mad about? Would I be mad if someone else made the same mistake? Am I being too hard on myself? Can I forgive myself and try harder next time?" The result of such questions is often forgiveness and laughter.

✺

Patience is the best remedy for every trouble.
TITUS MACCIUS PLAUTUS

Are you angry less often now than in the past?

When we think about anger, we might acknowledge one benefit of the peace journey. The better we know ourselves and the more time we try to spend in the reality of God's constant presence, the less angry we feel. Of course anger never goes away completely, but when we make understanding and love our priorities, we see people and situations differently. We might see attention-getting behavior as loneliness, violence as festering woundedness, dishonesty as poverty of the soul.

◎◎

Anger is one of the sinews of the soul;
he that wants it hath a maimed mind.
THOMAS FULLER

Who is your enemy?

Accepting the divinity of all creation demands a change in the way we do nearly everything. Throwing food away is the squandering of a gift. Chopping down a tree for no reason insults the earth. And thinking of people as enemies is no longer our *modus operandi*. When we know that folks who make us mad are loved by God as much as we are, when we know that God lives in them as much as in us, then instead of an enemy, we see a person in trouble. Instead of seeing rotten people, we see people doing rotten things.

Just as we can be at peace even in the midst of suffering, so too can we love in the midst of anger.

◎◎

God said: "I do not laugh at my enemies, because I wish to make it impossible for anyone to be my enemy. Therefore I identify myself with my enemy's own secret self."
THOMAS MERTON

Do you care what people think about you?

One of life's biggest peace stealers is vanity. If we're constantly worrying about how we look or how others will react to us, then we're not caught up in the beauty of life. What keeps people off dance floors? Not the fear of having a lousy time, but the fear of looking stupid. Take a vow today to have fun and forget about what people think of you.

☺☺

With regard to honour and dishonour the mean is proper pride, the excess is known as a sort of empty vanity, and the deficiency undue humility.

ARISTOTLE

*As you move along your peace journey,
do those you love fear the changes
they see in you?*

Some of the students I teach in college have been
away from formal education for many years. They have
husbands and wives, children, full-time jobs, and busy
lives. One experience they share is the fear their college studies evoke in their loved ones. These students
are learning new things, developing new attitudes and
tastes, gaining confidence and independence, and, of
course, bringing their newfangled, crazy ideas home
with them. The firm ground of old relationships suddenly seems shaky, and the students' loved ones get
into a big funk and even lash out sometimes.

Journeys, both educational and spiritual, can exact
a price. You may discover that your loved ones disapprove of your new ways of looking at things and your
quiet passion for life. These are ditches and washed-
out bridges on the peace route, and I wish I could
offer a formula to mend them, but I can't. I can only
say that one should patiently and lovingly navigate.

◎◎

*Taking a new step,
uttering a new word is what people fear most.*
FYODOR DOSTOYEVSKY

Echo question:
Remember Saint Paul's definition of love?

Actually, I guess this qualifies as seven "echo questions." As you've noticed, this book talks a lot about love, so it's good to remind ourselves what love is: being patient and kind; not being envious, boastful, arrogant, rude, selfish, irritable, resentful, narrow-minded, or stingy.

Of course, it's impossible to keep all of this in mind all the time, which is why love needs to be an "is," not a "do."

@@

When you love you wish to do things for.
You wish to sacrifice for. You wish to serve.
ERNEST HEMINGWAY

Do you try to win approval from others?

We all long for compliments and popularity. The problem is that acceptance based on facades creates tension within ourselves that just won't go away. Each time we turn around we have to put on one more mask to please people who might well accept us as we are if given the chance. We need to be ourselves and quit worrying about the consequences.

❂

Don't try to please everybody. It's like that fable about the man, the boy, and the donkey walking down the street. People pointed and said, isn't it terrible that the strong man is riding the donkey and making the small boy walk. So they changed places and people pointed and said, isn't that terrible that the strong young boy is riding the donkey and making that poor man walk. So they both got on the donkey, the donkey came to the bridge, exhausted, fell into the river and drowned. And of course the moral of the story is if you try to please everybody, you'll lose your donkey.

DONALD RUMSFELD

Can you say no?

Saying no is difficult. Most of us want to be helpful and to please our friends. Some of us are so sensitive that we say yes to phone solicitations and to kids selling candy bars at our door just to avoid disappointing somebody, but part of finding a spot on the cosmic dance floor is standing our ground. I know this sounds harsh, but often *no* is the kindest word to say for all concerned. Buying a candy bar, which you may not want, or agreeing to serve on one more committee, when you're already on three other committees, may seem kind at the moment, but if you're trying to cut back on sugar or simplify your life, it's best to say no.

☯☯

Just say "no."
NANCY REAGAN

Do you blame others when things go wrong?

Blaming is destructive because it serves mostly selfish purposes. If somebody else is to blame when we lose our keys or get a poor grade on an exam, then all we do is build a false sense of esteem. There are plenty of reasons to love ourselves; we don't need fake ones.

@@

Blame-all and Praise-all are two blockheads.
BENJAMIN FRANKLIN

Do you recognize signs that you should turn inward?

Charles, a friend of mine, once said, "There's no tricking my stomach." He's very spiritual, a person of great faith, but no matter how at peace he felt in his mind, he always knew that when his stomach was burning, something was bothering his mind or spirit.

Charles's upset stomach was a sign to him that, no matter how great things seemed, he needed to turn inward, to prayerfully, silently ask himself what was going on. My own sign is a specific stiffness in my neck.

The speed at which we live and work enables us to internalize our suffering without naming it. We think everything's okay, then we get a killer headache, intestinal irritation, insomnia, etc. As people seeking peace, we need to respect the body's suggestions that we stop, breathe, and peruse our days for thorns that keep snagging our spirit's fabric.

@⊚

Who's not sat tense before his own heart's curtain?
RAINER MARIA RILKE

Are you always getting behind?

Most people I know fall behind now and again, but always getting behind may be a sign of a person whose goals are scattered. If you are working on saying no when you should and focusing on things that are important to you, you'll find that it's easier to stay on top of your responsibilities. Do what you want to do and what you're good at—efficiency will slowly come to you.

@@

The rule is, jam tomorrow, and jam yesterday—
but never jam today.
LEWIS CARROLL

Can you spare a minute?

You'd be surprised at what you can accomplish with just sixty seconds. In sixty seconds you can probably do a quick pick up of your living room, or grunt through ten or twenty sit-ups, or wash a window, or bring a little peace to your day. As you can imagine, I believe that the last of these is the most valuable.

Often we assume that because we don't have much time to put into an enterprise we should abandon the effort altogether. Where spiritual peace is concerned, however, we can't afford not to use the minutes available to us to seek out pockets of God's presence. The next time you find yourself in the middle of a busy day, try to get alone for one minute, close your eyes, take several cleansing breaths, let go of the tension in your body, and rest with God. One minute, that's all. Watch the power those seconds can have for your day.

@@

Come to me, all you that are weary and are carrying heavy burdens, and I will give you rest.
MATTHEW 11:28

Do you "manage" stress?

Stress management: over the course of a year in the town I live in, there are as many workshops that tell us how to "control" our stress as there are corner bars— and we have a lot of corner bars in Erie, Pennsylvania. I've given a fair number of these workshops over the years, and the more I do them, the more I dislike them. It's as if we think that we can spend years tying our bodies, minds, and spirits into knots, and then unravel them all with a two-hour workshop.

To "manage" stress is perhaps a shortsighted endeavor, for we manage things that are always with us. What I think we want to do is not manage what stress we have, but to cultivate in our spirits the ability to stop choosing stress and start choosing faith.

I'm not dumb enough to suppose that we can make all stress go away, but I do think we can turn it from the Terminator to a ninety-eight-pound weakling. So let's not manage stress; let's select joy.

☙❧

. . . anxiety is the mark of spiritual insecurity.
THOMAS MERTON

Echo question:
What kinds of things are you praying for
these days?

I believe in talking to God, not because God should give us what we want, but because we need to say what's on our minds. Just as a child might say to a parent, "I know supper's in five minutes, but could I have some ice cream," we should empty our hearts in prayer. Still, once we're unburdened, we should long for God's will, which is the only thing that will really make us happy.

◎◎

Do not pray for easy lives.
Pray to be stronger men.
JOHN F. KENNEDY

Is the darkness light?

It's odd the way images contradict themselves. I have said many times that the Divine is light and life, and I have used the term "darkness" to suggest the feeling of being lost.

Yet what happens when we close our eyes? We see darkness, and most often it's in this state that we pray or meditate. To be sure, there is the deep night of suffering alone, but there is also the light of darkness that comes when we pull flesh over our eyes, breathe deeply, and open ourselves to God. In this sense, and for the moment of contemplation, the absence of light is the ultimate light.

@@

. . . there is a higher light still, not the light by which man "gives names" and forms concepts, with the aid of the active intelligence, but the dark light in which no names are given, in which God confronts man not through the medium of things, but in His own simplicity.

THOMAS MERTON

What is contemplation?

I've tried hard in this book not to "stage" questions; that is, I've avoided asking questions just so I can present flashy quotations. I'm cutting myself a break here, however, because I think Thomas Merton captures the nature of contemplation as many people try to practice it. As you engage in your own prayer/meditation, you might keep his words on your mind's end table.

@@

The union of the simple light of God with the simple light of man's spirit, in love, is contemplation. The two simplicities are one. They form, as it were, an emptiness in which there is no addition but rather the taking away of names, of forms, of content, of subject matter, of identities. In this meeting there is not so much a fusion of identities as a disappearance of identities.

THOMAS MERTON

How do you move toward interior silence?

I believe a regular practice of interior silence is crucial for spiritual peace. For this reason, I am devoting the next three meditations to contemplative prayer, a method of reaching silence. Perhaps you can borrow from it and adapt it to your needs.

Contemplative prayer has been written about at length by Basil Pennington and Thomas Keating, among others. It runs roughly like this: Set aside twenty to thirty minutes each day. Pick a comfortable, solitary place to sit down. Find something meaningful to read, Scripture or some work on spirituality per-haps, and read slowly for a few minutes. Then, close your eyes and think about what you've read. Soon your mind will start to drift, and that's good. Let it, as Merton puts it, "rest in the quiet expectancy of God." The goal then is to spend about twenty minutes in this state. More on "this state" in the next meditation.

☺☺

Contemplative prayer is a deep and simplified spiritual activity in which the mind and will rest in a unified and simple concentration upon God.
THOMAS MERTON

What is interior silence?

Since I can't get into anyone else's head, I can only describe my interior silence. First of all, it doesn't come quickly or easily. I do need to relax, read, and reflect for at least a few moments before I'm ready to settle into silence. What is the silence itself like? Actually, it can be pretty noisy. In the beginning, some of the things I need to get done, want to do, or worry about say, "John, here I am, think about me."

The object is not to concentrate on those ideas, but to let them float by like boats on a river. I don't try to "fight" them, but I visualize them just passing down the river of my consciousness and out of sight. As the moments pass (and after years of practice), the crowd of ideas thins and I do find interior silence, during which I think of nothing and simply rest in God's presence.

The next two meditations will consider techniques for maintaining silence.

◎◎

What you need most in this dark journey is an
unfaltering trust in the Divine guidance. . . .
THOMAS MERTON

How can you quiet the noise in your silence?

Trying to maintain interior silence for a couple of minutes can let you know how noisy your head can be. Troubles cry out in your mind. Longings come bubbling to the surface. Old sorrows you weren't even aware of revisit your heart. Answers to longstanding problems articulate themselves brilliantly.

Although these may be benefits of contemplative prayer, its primary purpose is to remain open to the presence of God, and so dwelling on any particular idea, no matter how rewarding, in the end closes that openness. The object then is *not* to focus on any one idea, but to usher ideas from your mind. I've already mentioned one way of doing so (ideas are boats floating by on a river). Another way is to repeat a focusing word or phrase in your mind any time an idea sticks to your silence. I've mentioned before that I say "God's peace" or "let go." You can think of such a phrase as gently leading the ideas away.

☺☺

It [the focusing word or "sacred word"] is chosen not for its content but for its intent. It is merely a pointer that expresses the direction of your inward movement toward the presence of God.
THOMAS KEATING

What if you can't find time for interior silence?

In short, you can't afford not to find time for the practice of silence. I know extraordinarily busy people who find time for contemplative prayer. Several people I know get up between 5 and 6 A.M. to pray. Some even fall asleep as they are praying, and that lets them know they need to rearrange priorities to get more sleep.

Most people I know practice contemplative prayer in the morning before getting into the day's demands, but you could wait until evening. The main point is that you make time in your day for a spiritual practice of silence. I suspect contemplative prayer presents a method compatible with the beliefs of most readers of this book, but if this way of silence doesn't suit you, please seek out another. The method isn't as important as the communion with the Divine.

෯෯

The butterfly counts not months but moments,
and has time enough.
RABINDRANATH TAGORE

Do you have a method of remembering things?

If you do a good job of remembering commitments and if you don't walk around feeling as if you're always forgetting something, you can probably skip this question. But if you're forgetful, it may not have occurred to you before that a mind cluttered with uncertainty about details is not at peace. The key to solving this problem is to develop a system for keeping track of what you need to get done each day. For what it's worth, I sit down for a few minutes each morning and write on a small index card my appointments from my calendar as well as all the things I want to get done. I never get everything done, but that's okay because writing out the list gives me a clear sense of what must be done today and what can wait. Then a couple of days a week I look up to three weeks ahead on my calendar and jot down tasks I need to do ahead of time (e.g., buying birthday presents before the day of the party). This system works for me. Find one that works for you and stick to it.

◎◎

"Submit to the rule you laid down."
ENGLISH PROVERB

Do you take responsibility for your life?

It's true that people do lots of things, good and bad, to affect our lives, but unless we assume primary responsibility for our circumstances (or at least for changing our circumstances if we don't like them), then we are powerless. When we do not see situations as *ours* to change, then we have no basis for acting. For example, a person who's been sexually abused as a child will continue to suffer without much hope until "victim" becomes "survivor," until the abused person decides that it is up to her or him to heal and grow. When such a person, or any person, says, "I have to take responsibility for my life," he or she is empowered. Others may be the source of our suffering, but we are to blame if we continue to suffer.

 co

*You have to pay your dues
if you wish to belong to the society
in which you live.*
EDITH HAMILTON

Have you made a mess of your life?

A number of people I know who are on peace journeys have told me that what made them aware of their spiritual needs was the mess they had made of their lives. Another thing they talk about is feeling cleansed. As they spent time praying, meditating, and contemplating their lives, they came to accept a miracle: it is possible to rise from the ashes of despair stronger and smarter than before. Although we have to deal with the individual messes we've made, we don't need to trudge through our days carrying a cargo of self-loathing. As God within and around us lifts that load, it disappears altogether.

☯

Forgiving presupposes remembering.
PAUL TILLICH

Would you jump out of the crowd?

I recently saw a television show about a study of crowd behavior. The research concluded that often individuals in crowds don't act when action is required. In short, if you keel over from a heart attack on a street corner, you'd be better off if only one person saw you than if fifty people were standing beside you. The reason: there's a weird group dynamic that causes indecisiveness and fear when the group is faced with a crisis. This is why we hear stories about a bunch of folks witnessing a beating and nobody helping out.

And so I ask again, would you jump out of the crowd? There's no nice, gentle answer to this one. You're on your own.

@@

Others can give you a name or a number,
but they can never tell you who you really are.
That is something you yourself
can only discover from within.
THOMAS MERTON

Can you accept painful mysteries?

Some horrific injustices and cruelties occur on the cosmic dance floor. As people of peace and strength, we honor people who suffer these horrors by witnessing what happens to them, acknowledging rather than forgetting that injustices occur, and by seeking ways to end cruelty.

As we dance, we need to remember just what people are capable of, *name* those who suffer, and *tell their stories*. As we sit in morning silence, surely somewhere in the world a knife is being put to flesh. Somewhere in the world, a child says, "Mom, I'm hungry." Somewhere in the world, an elderly man can't afford arthritis medicine.

In some ways, our voices are not only our own. They must speak for the mute multitudes who look in upon our peace and say, "Help!"

෨෨

My life does not belong to me.
RIGOBERTA MENCHU

Are you in love with shortcuts?

Sometimes shortcuts are fantastic. A friend of mine has a computer program that will figure out his taxes; all he needs to do is punch in the numbers and, boom, his completed tax return comes whizzing out of his ink-jet printer. For such matters, perhaps the quick and brainless way is best.

Many times, however, the shortcut mentality doesn't work. To learn to sing well, for example, you have to spend hours and hours just learning and practicing proper breathing. To read well, you have to read a lot. Let's face it, to do anything well, you have to pay the price of time and effort. To suppose otherwise leads to aggravation and disappointment.

@@

Don't learn the tricks of the trade.
Learn the trade.
ANONYMOUS

Do you spend more money than you have?

There's nothing inherently wrong with getting into debt, provided you pay back what you owe; however, the problem with debt is the psychological interest. Being in debt is stressful, and the more stress you have in your life, the harder it is to be at peace.

@@

Be not made a beggar by banqueting upon borrowing,
when thou hast nothing in thy purse.

ECCLESIASTICUS
FROM THE *APOCRYPHA*

*When somebody you love looks sad or angry,
do you assume you did something wrong?*

We often falsely assume that our loved ones' moods
and bad days are our fault and take their glum looks as
personal insults or reasons to feel guilty. How we over-
estimate our importance! If someone is not doing
well, we shouldn't suppose that we're responsible
until we ask. When we find out that we're not, we
need to fight the impulse of depriving our loved ones
of their moods. People usually get sad for a reason.
Real love is staying with people through their sadness,
not owning it ourselves or combating it.

@@

Faults are thick where love is thin.
JAMES HOWELL

Do you heed your own advice?

As with many questions in this book, this one deals with simple honesty and integrity. If you give advice that you're not willing to heed yourself, that means you are probably trying to control somebody else's suffering, which you cannot do, or you are not being yourself. Either way, you are not thinking peacefully.

๏๏

*Be wary of the man who urges an action
in which he himself incurs no risk.*
JOAQUIN SETANTI

Would you know a gift
if it bit you on the nose?

Yesterday I was feeling pretty stressed out, why's not important. I was driving along, my hands wrapped around the steering wheel, the rest of my body clenched. Then I turned a corner, and by God's grace, I saw the beauty of the day in which I was living. The sky was blue, not a perfect, deep blue, but a longing blue, just a bit of haze to it. The sky wished it could be bluer. I had my windows down, and the rush of air was making my hair stick up in the back. The trees were swelling with green.

The most important thing I did all day was accept the gift of that moment, when God called out to me in color and breeze. I've spent too much of my life seeing gifts only after they've passed by. Join me: let's see Divine offerings as they approach and stop getting these stupid teeth marks in our noses.

⊚⊘

He that shuns trifles must shun the world.
GEORGE CHAPMAN

Echo question:
Have you been given faith?

I've heard some people ask, "How do you get faith? I'd like to have some." Earlier in the book, I suggest that faith is necessary for spiritual peace, yet it's pretty hard to cultivate on your own. Where, then, can we go to find a trust in God that frees us to loosen our grip on life's controls?

Though it seems strange and paradoxical, the Lutheran and other Protestant denominations hold that faith itself is a gift of God, something we can't attain on our own. So if you're beating yourself up because you feel faithless, relax. When you go into your time of prayer and meditation, ask God for the gift of trust. Entertain the notion within yourself that faith is a free gift, which you don't merit by being good. It's just a gift.

☙

A man consists of the faith that is in him.
Whatever his faith is, he is.
BHAGAVADGITA

Can you visualize healing?

Do you wonder as I do about the potential of the human mind? Might it be possible some day to cure diseases by thinking about them in the right way? Right now the biofeedback technique has taught us that it is possible, for example, to use our mental control to raise the temperature of a certain area of the body and in this way to find relief from pain. Doesn't this suggest staggering possibilities?

Although we don't yet have the ability to use our intellects to heal all ills, we can find comfort by seeing in our minds the reality of God's healing in our lives. Particularly when I'm feeling my body rebelling against stress, I visualize God's healing light rising from within my body and encircling me from without. I don't do this in an effort to force God's will, but to "see" the reality that God doesn't want me to suffer from self-induced fear and sadness. In such cases, we are given the power of God to work toward healing ourselves.

᭸᭸

A rock pile ceases to be a rock pile the moment
a single man contemplates it, bearing within him
the image of a cathedral.
ANTOINE DE SAINT-EXUPÉRY

Do you eat wisely most of the time?

Eating wisely all of the time is just about impossible. Sometimes it's healthier to eat a sausage sandwich than to experience the stress of disappointing the person who served it up. The point is, we should try to practice good nutrition most of the time. Eating healthy should be the norm from which we deviate once in a while.

@@

Don't dig your grave with your knife and fork.
ENGLISH PROVERB

Are you willing to learn about nutrition?

Learning about nutrition isn't easy, but it's necessary. If your body is always feeling sluggish or pained because of a lousy diet, then you can't expect your mind and spirit to be at peace. It's true that reading labels for fat, sugar, sodium, and other dietary devils can be tedious, but after a while it becomes second nature. Besides, the benefits of a healthy diet are worth the trouble: increased energy, improved moods, and appropriate weight loss.

◎◎

Eat not to dullness; drink not to elevation.
BENJAMIN FRANKLIN

Are you willing to change your tastes?

To become healthy, you will probably have to adjust some of your tastes. If you love french fries and cheeseburgers on buttered buns, you'll just have to love them a little less often. If you hate vegetables, you'll have to get into the spirit of finding ones you like. The more stubborn you are about keeping your old tastes and the more reluctant you are to acquire new ones, the more trouble you'll have establishing a healthy diet.

☯

The true wisdom is to be always seasonable, and to change with a good grace in changing circumstances.
ROBERT LOUIS STEVENSON

245

Do you sleep soundly?

There are many reasons for poor sleep; one can be a mind that's not at peace. When we go to sleep, the troubling matters that we've been keeping a lid on all day can bubble over. The result is wakefulness. If you've been having trouble sleeping, one course of action might be to spend some waking time exploring the personal issues that have been bothering you. After doing so, you might also pray about your issues to God, who will gladly share them with you.

๏๏

In my younger days I heard someone, I forget who, remark, "Sell to the sleeping point." That is a gem of wisdom of the purest ray serene. When we are worried it is because our subconscious mind is trying to telegraph us some message of warning. The wisest course is to sell to the point where one stops worrying.

BERNARD M. BARUCH

Do you get enough sleep?

As with all physical discomforts, lack of sleep is a peace stealer. When we're not well rested, the simple problems we deal with every day become major crises. Living becomes a matter of surviving rather than thriving. If your lifestyle doesn't permit you enough sleep, look for things to eliminate.

⊚⊘

Rid yourself of . . . "the Thomas Edison syndrome." That's the belief that people who accomplish a lot do so because they get by with little sleep.
BUSINESS WEEK

Echo question:
Are you still worried about the future?

A friend of mine gave the address at a college gradua-
tion recently, and I asked him if he had been nervous.

"I was," he told me, "but the closer the time came
to give the speech, the more peaceful I felt. When I
was up there I really wasn't nervous at all."

Aren't most things in life this way? We fret and
tremble, then find that what we'd feared was not so
bad in the end. Aside from being foolish, getting all
wrapped up in thinking about the future is an insult to
faith.

ෙ෨

We steal if we touch tomorrow.
It is God's.
HENRY WARD BEECHER

Is the world full of turtles,
and are you one of them?

Here is a simple but I hope eye-opening exercise: The next time you are in a public place (especially at work), take note of the way people carry their necks and shoulders. It is indicative of today's stress level that, as a matter of course, folks walk around as if they were turtles about to retreat into their shells. Perhaps we all feel as if our heads are on the chopping blocks of a downsizing world.

It's amazing what this one little observation can do for your health. Develop the habit of doing periodic shoulder checks throughout the day, especially if you have a desk job. If you notice that your shoulders seem pinned to your earlobes, take a deep breath, sit up straight, and relax your shoulders. Watch how many headaches you can avoid.

✪✪

This is, I think, very much the Age of Anxiety,
the age of the neurosis, because along with so much
that weighs on our minds there is perhaps
even more that grates on our nerves.
LOUIS KRONENBERGER

Do you have fun creating things?

It's not enough for us to simply survive this life. As human beings we need to demonstrate our beauty through creation. What we create can be varied and unpredictable. A nicely organized plant window, a poem, or a good meal can be an expression of who we are. The key is to see our lives and actions as creations to celebrate.

@@

You must create your own world.
I am responsible for my world.
LOUISE NEVELSON

Do you choose boredom,
or does it choose you?

Lots of people get bored once in a while; occasional boredom can actually be a luxury if we choose to make room for nothingness in our schedules. Sometimes, however, our ennui takes on a life of its own, and we feel powerless to climb out of it. Unless, of course, clinical depression is an issue, we don't need to allow boredom to choose us. What we need to do is broaden our scope of activities.

I realize that what I'm saying here echoes the old-fashioned keep-busy philosophy, but I believe there's a measure of truth in it. The world is bursting with things to do, simple things like going on a walk and watching for different kinds of birds, cerebral things like journaling, purposeful things like visiting people in the hospital. The point is, if we're bored, it should be because we choose to be, not because we are forced to be.

◎◎

Boredom: the desire for desires.
LEO TOLSTOY

Echo question:
Have you physically challenged yourself yet?

One of the beauties of the spiritual journey is that things you once figured were impossible are now possible. By opening yourself up to the Divine presence, you may have felt a sense of calm that you hadn't felt before. You may also have found reserves of patience and compassion you hadn't known were there.

I believe similar discoveries are possible where our bodies are concerned. True, some people do have major physical limitations, but most of us are capable of more than we think we are. Consider the possibility of beginning an exercise program in which you challenge yourself from time to time.

◎◎

It is better to wear out than to rust out.
RICHARD CUMBERLAND

Are you educating yourself about spirituality / religions?

Some folks are afraid of learning about religion and philosophies because they think they might pick up new and dangerous ideas that will lead them astray. The fear for people of my generation was that we might fall prey to a cult. Although such things do happen occasionally, seeking out new perspectives on spirituality and religion is a necessary part of the peace journey. Clearly the danger of being sealed off from influences outside our own is greater than the danger of being open.

For example, without Christianity's dialogue with Zen Buddhism, the meditative quality of prayer practiced by ancient Christian mystics might never have been rediscovered and integrated into the contemplative prayer movement. In this case, non-Christians helped Christians listen to their own heritage.

As people seeking peace, we should listen to the voices of God's children who come from various traditions, respect the ways in which they can teach us, and trust the God within us to discern the helpful from the destructive.

*Education, properly understood,
is that which teaches discernment.*
JOSEPH ROUX

Can you create solitude?

In a busy life, solitude must be created. It must be looked for and seized. It must be perceived. For example, let's say that your drive home from work is one of the few quiet times you have each day. You can create solitude in this perhaps brief and even demanding space by choosing to play either soothing music or no music at all. You can focus on limited relaxation during driving. You can pray or sing. If you create and practice solitude within a particular setting or time frame, soon you will enjoy the peace you'd assumed you were too busy to find.

๑๑

Cultivate solitude and quiet and a few sincere friends,
rather than mob merriment, noise and thousands of
nodding acquaintances.
WILLIAM POWELL

Do you love to laugh?

As is mentioned earlier in this book, statues of Buddha are usually fat, bald, and either laughing or wearing a silly grin. I suspect Buddha is laughing at the joy of living, the joy of what is, the joy of the cosmic dance. If you don't like to laugh, take notice of what your body feels like after you've had a good laugh. A belly laugh refreshes, invigorates, and relieves pressure. God has given us laughter, and we should enjoy it often.

∾∾

Frame your mind to mirth and merriment,
Which bars a thousand harms and lengthens life.
WILLIAM SHAKESPEARE

Can you laugh at yourself?

When we've made a mistake, we have a choice: we can either laugh or beat ourselves up. The only thing we accomplish by the latter is lowering our self-esteem and raising our blood pressure; by laughing at ourselves we probably lower our blood pressure, but more important, we grant to ourselves the gentleness and good humor that we hope others will give to us. Laughing at ourselves is loving and kind—and a lot more fun than hollering.

☺☺

Laugh at yourself first,
before anyone else can.
ELSA MAXWELL

Are you a fidgety child?

Have you ever seen a child who just won't sit still? You know the child is tired, hungry, sick, unhappy, and if only he or she would climb up on Mom's lap and rest, things would get better in a skinny minute. The challenge, of course, is to lasso the kid.

I wonder if God sees us as fidgety children sometimes, children who, in the words of the poet James Wright, "rush ceaselessly in place." The next time you're rushing about, zooming from one episode of panic to another, ask yourself if you're not being a child of God with ants in your pants. If you are, have a good laugh, sit still, and open yourself to the Divine presence.

@@

Nothing gives rest but the sincere search for truth.
BLAISE PASCAL

Do you know that comedy is painful?

Although a humorous and lighthearted approach to life is healthy, we need to recognize the limits of humor as well as its very nature. Have you ever noticed how laughing and crying are a lot alike? Sometimes the two get mixed up and come out together. Sometimes we laugh until we cry. Sometimes it's hard to tell whether somebody is laughing or crying. The two are so close because they usually come from the same source. Jokes are insulting. Slapstick humor is physically painful. Bloopers are embarrassing. It's good to laugh loudly and often, but we also need to realize when laughing causes more pain than it relieves.

@@

Comedy is pain.
PAUL IDDINGS

Are you humble?

The more peaceful you become, the more you care about other people. This is a sign of God reaching through you to support and heal. Being humble isn't discarding our accomplishments; it's being so full of love and compassion that we are minimized and the "God in us" is maximized.

๏๏

Always remember there are two types of people in this world. Those who come into a room and say, "Well, here I am!" and those who come in and say, "Ah, there you are!"

FREDERICK L. COLLINS

Do you care if you get credit for your accomplishments?

We're conditioned to assume that everything has a price tag. Sometimes this conditioning is correct. If we have a fancy car, it's just that we make hefty payments. If we borrow money from a friend, we ought to pay it back. But what if we do something special and don't get recognized? We feel cheated, slighted. We need to remember that there is a beauty in doing good work that lies in the process, not in the recognition. The more insulted we feel at not getting credit, the more insecure we are about our own worth. Think of yourself as filled with God's goodness and as recognized by God, even when others take you for granted. Work on, filled with and inspired by God's wisdom and love.

〰️

*Envie not greatness; for thou mak'st thereby
Thyself the worse, and so the distance greater.*
GEORGE HERBERT

Can you swim smoothly in a tidal wave?

With the contemporary trend of downsizing in business comes fewer people wearing more hats. In fact, jump into lots of business conversations, and you'll hear something like, "Yes, well, Steve, one of the hats I wear is Director of Grant Proposal Writing for Plastics Research." Translation: "Director of Grant Proposal Writing for Plastics Research is one of the roles I'm supposed to fill on top of five others. I actually run around putting out fires as they break out."

People trying to cultivate spiritual peace need to avoid beating themselves up because they are asked to do more than is possible, desirable, or healthy. Of course, leaving situations like the one I described might be an option, but when it isn't, it's crucial to do your best without allowing yourself to feel the weight of responsibility for things that don't get done. We all would like to think we're superhuman, but nobody I know of can swim in a tidal wave. Sometimes keeping your head above water is a victory.

⚭

He that is everywhere is nowhere.
THOMAS FULLER, M.D.

Do you see the world through the eyes of love?

The next time you hear people going on and on about how the poor are responsible for their own suffering, about how immigrants crowding our cities ought to go back where they came from, or about how people on welfare ought to get jobs, listen to the anger in their voices. Each time you see a situation of which you disapprove, ask yourself, "How would I feel if the person I loved most in the world were in that position?" Each time you begin to condemn, give in to the love that is in you. The world may contain a lot of suffering, but you can be a force of healing and understanding by opening your heart.

ⓒⓔ

Let no one underestimate the need of pity.
We live in a stony universe whose hard,
brilliant forces rage fiercely.
THEODORE DREISER

Echo question:
Have you fallen in love with mysteries?

A friend and I were talking about our lives. She was going through a crisis, and as she finished telling me how she was feeling, I told her about the struggles of which I write in the introduction to this book. I told her about how sad I was, how filled with longing.

"What were you longing for?" she asked.

"I had no idea then," I told her, "but now I think I was longing for God."

We talked some more. I said that, for me, longing never quite goes away, but the more I open myself up to the Divine presence, the more that staggering echo within myself quiets down. I don't know how this happens, but it does.

I find myself dancing these days in the mystery of the presence that answers questions with better questions, that makes the full spirit light, that enlightens the mind in dark prayer. Just as answers give the muscles and mind rest, mysteries make the spirit weightless and singing.

◎◎

One doesn't discover new lands without consenting to lose sight of the shore for a very long time.
ANDRÉ GIDE

What is your responsibility to peace?

In the United States we often hear people speak of their rights, but seldom of their responsibilities. I would like to suggest that, as a person on the peace journey, you have a responsibility (a privilege, actually) to nurture peace among and within others. How can you do so? To tell the truth, going around talking about peace will probably get you a reputation for being weird.

The best way to spread peace is to live out your journey visibly. Whatever flaws you might have, you can offer peace to others in small ways: a "hello" and a smile; a cup of coffee; a pat on the shoulder, a "how are you" that rings true. In these ways and, of course, in much larger ways as well, we can be the presence of God to those around us. Peace should resonate in our voices, shimmer in our laughter, and calm those we touch.

⊚⊚

You may be the only Bible some person ever reads.
WILLIAM J. TOMS

Can you flip confrontation?

What's the opposite of *confrontation?* Let's take the word apart and see what happens. "Con" is a prefix that means "against." I can suggest two meanings for "front" that seem appropriate: one would be "before, as opposed to behind"; and two would be "a military line."

So with confrontation, you are against a person in an obvious and perhaps threatening fashion. The question is, is there an alternative to confrontation? I have one to suggest. The opposite of confrontation as I've presented it here would be to be "for" a person, to be "behind" her or him in a "peaceful fashion."

Sound idealistic? The next time you feel the need to confront somebody, ask yourself, "Would explaining my common ground with this person serve the same function as confrontation? Would being peaceful work in this case?" You'll be amazed at how often you can flip confrontation.

◎◎

The snappish cur always has torn ears.
FRENCH PROVERB

Do you worry about what to say?

More times in my life than I'd care to admit, I remained silent when I should have spoken. The reasons ranged from social tension, to a fear of making matters worse, to a simple inability to find the right words. All of these reasons have one thing in common: they point to an underlying attempt to control. If I fear social tension, then I want to calm the situation. If I'm worried about making matters worse, then chances are I'm trying to make them better. If I can't find the right words, then I'm probably searching for words that will lead the situation one way or another.

If we speak out of genuine love and in an attempt to offer our presence to others, we don't need to worry so much about saying the right thing. The situations we speak to are what they are, and all we should try to do is bring a compassionate presence to them.

@@

A man is hid under his tongue.
ALI IBN-ABI-TALIB

Are you able to really say "good-bye"?

Much of the peace journey consists of openings; in fact, the central image of healthy spirituality might well be arms open wide to others and the gifts of the world. Still, there are moments when we need to acknowledge tasks of closure and bring to them love and integrity. When a loved one is dying, when friends are leaving for good, when we move away from somewhere we love, we should have the courage to say ending words and not pretend that everything's okeydokey.

When we fail to say "good-bye" with sincerity and acknowledge the sorrow of departures, we sacrifice the joy woven through even our most bitter moments: the Divine promise of resurrection. Even as weeping rises in our throats, a smile is already forming on our lips. We know that we and those we love are not living a "start" and "finish," but a journey through mountains, valleys, and great canyons when we walk together and hear the endless echoes of promises: "I am with you always"; "my peace I give you"; "I will raise you up."

⊚⊚

Ever has it been that love knows not its own
depth until the hour of separation.
KAHLIL GIBRAN

Do you worry that your giving is insignificant?

Once when I was in charge of social ministry at a church, a woman called to ask if she could have some money for food. I had money in my budget, so I managed to get her a check. The next day I told my friend Roy about my doubts. "I'm not sure what good it did," I said. "She'll probably be out of food again in a few days anyway, if she even bought food in the first place."

Since Roy is the pastor of an urban congregation, he was able to give me a few pointers on how to most effectively provide for people who live a day or two away from homelessness. His final words to me, however, were consoling, encouraging: "Don't worry," he said. "When Christ fed the thousands, they might have been hungry the next day, too, or maybe they threw the food away, but for that day, he knew they could choose to eat."

The point: sometimes our gift seems awkwardly given and about as meaningful as a nickel flipped into the Grand Canyon, but that nickel might mean, "I've got just enough now to get a quart of milk; that'll get me through to the day after tomorrow."

※

It is better to light a candle than to curse the darkness.
CHINESE PROVERB

*Do you worry about why
people need your help?*

When we worry about *why* people need our help, we tend to judge, which is not our job. This is not to say, however, that we need to be totally blind to causes, but when we concern ourselves more with causes than with suffering, we're trying to do God's work. God never said, "Love your neighbor as you love yourself—provided your neighbor hasn't done anything wrong." God's love to us is unconditional *(agape)*. We should imitate it.

⊚⊚

*When you see a man in distress,
recognize him as a fellow man.*
SENECA

Do you minimize other people's suffering?

I don't for a moment suspect that you as a reader of this book would knowingly minimize anyone's suffering. I'm talking here about the times when we try to encourage people and unwittingly imply that what they're going through doesn't add up to much. In an honest effort to make somebody feel better, we say things like "Everything will be okay," "Chin up," and "There are plenty of fish in the sea." What we don't realize is that such messages are heard as "You shouldn't be feeling bad." Better to say "I'm sorry you're suffering," or "I'm with you," or "I want to help you."

@@

We hand folks over to God's mercy,
and show none ourselves.
GEORGE ELIOT

Is listening enough?

The world is full of people who want to give advice, but a good listener is rare. When people want to talk, they seldom want help; they want to be heard, really heard. Telling others how to solve their problems is actually pretty insulting; moreover, it's usually a reflection of the helper's impulse to control the world. But to listen, to be present to a person in pain, this is possible, pure, honest. Advice is good when requested. Listening is usually enough.

❦

Give us grace to listen well.
JOHN KEBLE

When you give,
do you expect something in return?

Sometimes we'll do a favor for a friend and truly believe that we expect nothing in return. Then, at a later date, when the friend is unable to grant us a favor, we're bugged. "Heck," we say, "I helped her out, and now where is she when I need her?" Although we're justified in feeling this way, such feelings do betray our motives. We almost always expect something in return for kindness. Letting go of our sense of fairness is difficult, but our acts of kindness mean nothing if we keep track of them in our minds.

୨୨

We should give as we would receive,
cheerfully, quickly, and without hesitation,
for there is no grace in a benefit that
sticks to the fingers.
SENECA

Are you able to accept kindness?

We've all heard the old saying, "It is better to give than to receive." True enough, but many of us need to work on our receiving skills. As conscientious people we're so concerned about not troubling others that we don't receive very graciously. What we don't realize is that letting others give to us is itself a gift. Showing appreciation for kindness is a way of building up those we love.

๑๑

Don't be a stingy receiver.
EDGAR DALE

Are you true to your beliefs?

As long as we live with integrity, and as long as our behavior doesn't hurt anybody else or ourselves, then we shouldn't feel pressure to live as society says we ought to live. However, sometimes that pressure is tough to deal with, so tough that we pretend to live out one life publicly while we live out another privately. The fact is, we don't need to announce our lifestyles to the world; privacy is our right. What we shouldn't do is say one thing and do the opposite—and not primarily because dishonesty is wrong, but because it makes us worry about appearances rather than living, and that for me is the greater sin.

☺☺

You should not live one way in private,
another in public.
PUBLILIUS SYRUS

Echo question:
Are you being light and life for others?

When I'm trying to decide whether I should do something in particular, I ask myself a standard question: As much as is possible, is this action going to lead to light and life? For me, this question really cuts through a lot of nonsense. Life is full of tough calls, but when decisions are made based on this question, self-interest and vanity have to be put aside.

If our actions do not *bring* light and life, then we can't claim to *be* light and life for others.

⊚∅

To give and then not feel that one has given
is the very best of all ways of giving.
SIR MAX BEERBOHM

Echo question:
Do you recognize poverty?

The philosophy of this book is that, most likely, poverty among people who can afford to go into a bookstore and buy a book is mostly a thing of the mind. It's important to recognize, however, that much economic poverty is profound, and in this world of wealth, inexcusable.

The danger in embracing the notion that poverty is a state of mind is that we somehow hold the poor responsible for their own poverty. We might also release ourselves from the responsibility to reach out with our energy and resources to address the needs of millions of our brothers and sisters who suffer.

The poverty of the mind is entirely different from severe economic poverty. For the former, we should open our spirits to the wealth of God. For the latter, our world should be ashamed.

◎◎

Poverty is very good in poems,
but it is very bad in a house.
It is very good in maxims and in sermons,
but it is very bad in practical life.
HENRY WARD BEECHER

Do you know when it's time to hit the eject button?

In a famous scandal of recent years, accountants in a large corporation falsified records to make losses appear to be profits. At first the motive was to buy the founder some time to get finances back on track; however, within a year or so the fraud had gotten entirely away from them. What at first was a sincere attempt on the accountants' part to be loyal team players turned into criminal activity, for which some went to jail.

It's easy to say that the accountants should have known better, but if we search ourselves, we can see the potential for falling into such a trap. The world can be a mire of half-truths and debatable realities. When does covering for a friend turn into a lie? When does massaging the numbers turn from "presentation" to deception?

There's no right answer, but there is a technique to help discern right from wrong. Pretend you are an outsider looking at yourself. At what moment would you say, "Eject"? When would you say, "Have courage. Do the right thing"?

@@

When things go wrong, don't go with them.
ANONYMOUS

Do you always worry about consequences?

Consequences are generally of concern to a person who's worried about what to *do* rather than what to *be*. If our actions grow out of who we are, then decision making becomes simpler than if we're always testing the wind to see what might result from our actions. For example, befriending a co-worker who just doesn't fit in might cost you the admiration of some colleagues, but if you hope to *be* love, then you don't have the luxury of worrying about the cost.

◎◎

People should think less about what they ought to do,
and more about what they ought to be.
MEISTER ECKHART

Echo question:
Are you still afraid to fail?

The further along the peace path one travels, the less one worries about failure. Why? Because when we try to make loving, patient decisions and when we claim the self-respect due us by the Divine indwelling, our failures are honest and noble. In this way, mistakes are sweetly sad, beautiful really, for in them we can see the purity of motives in people who long for peace. When good spirits try hard, there is no failure, only unpredictable results.

☺☺

*The young [and maybe not so young] think that
failure is the Siberian end of the line, banishment
from all the living, and tend to do what I then did—
which was to hide.*
JAMES BALDWIN

Is "tomorrow another day"?

As a kid, I hated the annual showing of *Gone with the Wind*; never did I realize that Scarlett O'Hara was offering me a pithy homily I'd come back to years later. The truth is, Scarlett had a bit of wisdom in her.

Although we can never leave our pasts behind us entirely, nor should we want to, we shouldn't constantly let ourselves get psyched out by yesterday. For example, it's unhealthy to say to ourselves, "I didn't eat right yesterday. I'll screw up today for sure."

Not true. We don't have to assume that yesterday defines today. In fact, for Christians, the resurrection carries with it the potential for *earthly* renewal. After all, if the dead can rise, maybe we can break the cycles we assume are permanent.

೦⊚

We know what we are,
but know not what we may be.
WILLIAM SHAKESPEARE

Are you disappointed that life doesn't get easier as you get older?

In truth, life has its tough periods, but overall life keeps presenting us with new and painful challenges. What can make life seem especially hard is when we live under the illusion that things are going to get easier for us if we can only hang in there. As we get older and find that life just stays hard, we can become embittered. M. Scott Peck has some good advice on this subject. In *The Road Less Traveled* he suggests accepting the difficult nature of life is helpful in dealing with suffering. We know that being human is a tough job and so are not surprised when faced with painful circumstances.

๛

Life is difficult.
M. SCOTT PECK

Is there joy in your sadness?

We're often told that we are the masters of our own destiny. There is some truth in this statement, in that we exert some control over many aspects of our lives. But when we overzealously embrace this philosophy, we experience despair if our destiny takes a sour turn. We blame ourselves.

One of the blessings of accepting life as it presents itself to us—rather than trying to doggedly control every experience—is that we open a window to joy in the midst of sadness. Even as we are suffering, we are able to see joy. As we are healing, we feel the first moisture of the joy storm approaching.

As part of life's weather, sadness passes, just as clouds move across the sky, unburden themselves on the earth, and form again. True, some profound pain never quite goes away, and this too is life's climate at work.

What a blessing this journey is. Dawn is visible on the horizon as we walk through the darkest, most bitter nights.

@@

In time of trouble avert not thy face from hope,
for the soft marrow abideth in the hard bone.
HAFIZ

Have your "oughts" turned to "mays"?

Elsewhere in this book I quote Gandhi, who, when asked if he ever intended to take a vacation from his grueling schedule, said, "I am always on vacation." The reason I suspect he was able to say this was that most of the "oughts" in his life had turned to "mays"; in other words, he viewed obligations as privileges.

I believe it can be this way with the spiritual journey. At some point, the patience and compassion we feel obliged to show others simply becomes the way we want to be. How wonderful it is to be the face of the Divine to those who need comfort. How calming to say words of healing to the sick.

I don't want to pretend here that loving others is always easy, but I do know that our spirits come to depend on the kindness we offer those around us.

@@

Alas, when duty grows thy law,
enjoyment fades away.
FRIEDRICH VON SCHILLER

Echo question:
Are you working to accept others
for who they are?

I believe it is possible to change many things about ourselves; it's tough to say just what we can change with God's help and what's pretty much fixed. For those of us on the peace journey, the issue of what's changeable and what's not can be a distraction; we need to focus on offering love, abundantly and foolishly, and know that changes we hope for may not materialize. When those we love can't change, we hear the challenge to love anyway. This is not to say, of course, that we should accept every situation. For example, the spouse who can't help sleeping around probably should not be a spouse anymore. The point is, love that demands changes of nature isn't really love.

◎◎

It is when we try to grapple with another man's
intimate need that we perceive how incomprehensible,
wavering, and misty are the beings that share with us
the sight of the stars and the warmth of the sun.
JOSEPH CONRAD

Can you say, "I love you"?

For men, at least, it's getting easier to say "I love you."
Still, there are lots of people we love whom we never
say those words to. Of course, we shouldn't all walk
around whispering "I love you" to each other. The
words become cheap after a while. But let's not avoid
talking about love when we need to, like when a
friendship is on the line, or when a loved one is feeling
unloved, or when a child feels alone.

@@

*One of our greatest learning tasks
is how to give and receive love.*
UNKNOWN

Do you try to articulate your feelings?

Words are powerful. Once you utter a truth about yourself, it's hard to turn back; this is why we're afraid to put our feelings into words. What if our feelings tell us something disturbing about ourselves? The problem is, the disturbing thing doesn't go away in silence; it just haunts us in other ways—lost sleep, headaches, ulcers. Best to work at *saying* what's on your mind, best to shape it, work with it, know it. Once feelings have words, they can be dealt with. Feelings without words eventually weigh upon the heart and slow down your cosmic dancing.

◎◎

As best you can, stare the truth in the face.
RICHARD VON WEIZACKER

Do you complain a lot?

"Wait a minute," you might be saying to yourself. "He just told us to talk about our feelings, and now he's asking if we complain a lot." Right, we do need to say what's on our minds, but when what's on our minds is often negative, we need to look at our minds. When we complain all the time, we're focused on ourselves. We think we have a heavier burden to bear than others and the world ought to pay attention to us. Remember, we can't have peace by stealing others' peace.

@@

The first lesson of life is to burn our own smoke;
that is, not to inflict on outsiders our
personal sorrows and petty morbidness,
not to keep thinking of ourselves as exceptional cases.
JAMES RUSSELL LOWELL

Do you need to just get on with your life?

My friend Tim and I were talking about an issue that I've been dealing with for about six or seven years. "I still haven't resolved this," I told him.

Then he said, "Don't you think it's about time you moved on anyway?" After talking to him for a while, I got his point. What he was suggesting was that I acknowledge that I'm not quite done dealing with the issue, but that maybe I should just get on with my life and come back to it later.

This simple suggestion was a revelation to me. Just as a writer might skip over a difficult chapter of a book and come back to it later, so any person *might* be able to table a painful matter and come back to it later. I'm not sure this is always possible, but it's comforting to know that an issue isn't going anywhere and that you can rest for a while and dwell on it some other time.

◎◎

To not go back is somewhat to advance,
And men must walk, at least, before they can dance.
ALEXANDER POPE

Do you take stock?

One of the premises of this book is that the peace journey is circular. There really isn't an ending to it, and we keep relearning and reinterpreting the same terrain; however, it is useful from time to time to be linear, to ask, "Where have I been? How far have I traveled?"

It's gratifying to see progress, to note some fears overcome, some troubling issues perhaps put to rest, some talents developed, some gifts given and received. Today, take a moment and look honestly at where you've been and how far you've traveled. Celebrate the distance.

☙❧

No single event can awaken within us
a stranger totally unknown to us.
To live is to be slowly born.
ANTOINE DE SAINT-EXUPÉRY

Does lust make you feel guilty?

Many people in my generation and especially my parents' generation grew up thinking that the only thing more sinful than having sexual thoughts was acting upon them. When I was around thirteen or fourteen years old, a friend said to me (I swear!), "I have to stop doing 'it.' I've got pimples all over the place."

More than twenty years later, I laugh, but I do remember feeling sick to my stomach and guilty as heck about my sexual feelings when I was a kid—and I know I'm not alone in this. Many of us carry these attitudes with us still, though intellectually we know better.

Feeling guilty about sexuality can be a real drag on spiritual peace, for when we feel sick about a natural part of physical life, we distance ourselves from what we are. If *all* we think about is sex, I suppose that's a problem. Otherwise, we needn't feel guilty for being human and having human desires.

☻

On the brink of being satiated,
desire still appears infinite.
JEAN ROSTAND

Can you assert yourself when necessary?

My wife has taught me, after many years of being a wimp, that sometimes I have to stand up for myself. I was the sort who hated to return merchandise to stores for fear of causing trouble, who *never* questioned a repair bill, who wouldn't think of promoting myself and my abilities. I finally learned to recognize when it was fair and proper for me to either gripe or toot my own horn. The key is not to be trampled upon unfairly for the sake of keeping the peace. Being humble and unselfish is vital to spiritual peace, but at some point silence becomes dysfunction.

◎◉

Promote yourself but do not demote another.
ISRAEL SALANTER

Are you willing to make the tough call?

For most of this book I have promoted healing, silence, reconciliation; however, we all have to recognize the exceptions to general rules. At some point, when friendships become abusive, we may have to distance ourselves. When loved ones are destroying themselves, we may have to risk hurting their feelings by insisting that they get help.

Sometimes, out of love for others and ourselves, we are forced to make tough, unpopular calls. That's okay; people of peace shouldn't be concerned about winning popularity contests, but about following the lead of a loving conscience.

⊙⊚

He only may chastise who loves.
RABINDRANATH TAGORE

Do you enable habitual suffering?

Let's face it, some folks seem to enjoy suffering or at least use suffering as a way to pass the time. As far into this book as you are by now, you know I'm a sucker for sympathy. However, it's important to acknowledge that some people may use suffering as a manipulative strategy.

In such cases, we need to pay attention to the person without validating the suffering. Getting caught up in false suffering clogs up our peace unnecessarily and, more importantly, enables unhealthy behavior in others. It is possible to be present to the "sufferer" without saying and doing things that encourage her or him to prolong the self-indulgence.

Of course, to take this uncharacteristic course, we must be sure of ourselves and others. I see such instances as rare, but significant to mention lest compassion be taken for stupidity.

ᘏᕔ

Sacrifice not thy heart upon every altar.
THOMAS FULLER

Are you the answer?

A phrase that needs to be on the tongue of the compassionate person is, "I'm not the answer to your problem." As people eager to walk with others on the road to peace, we sometimes confuse our need to care with our need to resolve. True, it can be torture to witness suffering without being able to end it, but it's a fact that, no matter how wise or talented we fancy ourselves to be, more often than not we aren't the answer to our loved one's problems.

Often there is no "answer." It's strangely calming to our spirits when we recognize that we're not responsible for fixing all problems, only for abiding with people who endure them.

❦

The heart errs like the head;
its errors are not any the less fatal,
and we have more trouble
getting free of them
because of their sweetness.
ANATOLE FRANCE

Do you try to find balance?

Balance is hard to attain. We try so hard to give to others that we completely forget ourselves. We work so much at developing our minds that we forget our bodies. We love so abundantly that we don't find a way to deal with anger. We desperately need to function in a state of questioning, to watch for neglecting one need entirely to fulfill another. In all things we need to find balance.

◎◎

The truth is that some creatures go before and others
  follow behind,
Some breathe one way, and others breathe another,
Some feel strong, and others feel weak,
Some like constructing and others like destroying.
This is why the sage has nothing to do with the excessive,
  the extravagant, or with being exalted.

LAO-TZU

Do you nourish your body with balance?

Let's face it, existence is confusing. There are so many variables that can influence our state of mind and body that we just can't keep track of them all. One of the most tempting things to overlook is the effect the body has on the mind. We feel sluggish at 3 P.M. and forget that maybe it's because we had a Reuben, onion rings, a chocolate milk shake, and a fat slice of triple-chocolate pie for lunch. Or we feel really unglued as we watch some schmaltzy television commercial that we usually laugh at and forget that we've been operating on four hours sleep per night for the last week.

The key here is not to get obsessive about sleep, diet, and exercise, but always to strive for balance in the way we treat our bodies or, at the very least, acknowledge the power of our bodies to affect our state of mind.

⊚⊚

If the mind, which rules the body, ever forgets itself
so far as to trample upon its slave, the slave is
never generous enough to forgive the injury;
but will rise and smite its oppressor.
HENRY WADSWORTH LONGFELLOW

Is there balance in your friendships?

I suppose the clichés about friendships are all more or less true. Yes: friendships take work; communication is the key to friendship; friends need to be tolerant of one another. The problem is, sometimes friendships fall out of balance or they're never balanced to begin with. This is a problem because I think most of us expect "friendships" to be reasonably balanced, with both people giving as much as taking.

A difficulty for people on the peace journey is that they tend to attract needy personalities (i.e., people who always seem to be in crisis or who are carrying lots of heavy baggage). Having lots of these relationships is draining, not necessarily because we're not able to offer support, but because we wait for a reciprocity that never materializes. Of course, we should love those who need our love, but we also need to define for ourselves the basis of our relationships and to seek out balanced friendships.

◎◎

*Friendship is a strong and habitual inclination
in two persons to promote the good
and happiness of one another.*
EUSTACE BUDGELL

Are you emotionally balanced?

An emotion that dominates our personalities is like a health condition that rules our bodies. For example, a person who gains a lot of weight around the middle might for the sake of physical health try to slim down; however, a person who is painfully pessimistic might simply say, "Hey, this is the way I am. Besides, people don't change."

Any one negative emotion that serves as a rudder constitutes a spiritual and mental health concern. If we're behaving one way all of the time, we ought to ask ourselves why—and perhaps also ask someone we trust why as well.

@@

People seem not to see that their opinion of the world is also a confession of character.
RALPH WALDO EMERSON

Is your journey balanced?

When my sister was in college she dated a guy I'll call Steve, a devout Christian. I can't remember Steve's major anymore, but he wanted to be either a dentist or a pastor and couldn't decide what to do. He told my sister that he was going to wait for God to tell him what to do. So preoccupied was he with listening that he became stagnant and depressed.

I'm not sure how Steve's story turned out, but I always think of him when I'm trying to discern God's will for my own life. The conclusion I've come to is that it's always a struggle to know what God would have us do. Sometimes I think God wants us to decide. The best we can do is strive for a balanced faith in which we always prayerfully listen but also act, knowing that we are doing the best we can and trying to be good.

◍◍

Faith embraces itself and the doubt about itself.
PAUL TILLICH

Can you say, "What's important here?"

In any one situation, a dozen things may present themselves as priorities. For example, dirty dishes may be in the sink, crumbs on the carpet, the dog's nose marks on the windows, and a child saying, "Come here a minute, Dad." If we say to any of the first three, "I'll get to you later," no harm is done. You can't hurt a plate. But if the child is being sincere, then you can't keep saying, "I'll get to you later."

Priorities are tough to discern when one is layered atop another, but it's precisely at the moment when we're feeling overwhelmed, when we have absolutely no time to spare, that we must pause and ask, "What's important here?" If we breathe, listen to God's silent voice, often we can hear the answer rising in us.

◎◎

A fool sees not the same tree that a wise man sees.
WILLIAM BLAKE ·

Do you take the easy way out sometimes?

The journey toward peace can seem awfully serious sometimes. We know that we need to love, show compassion, live with honesty and integrity, and those are demanding obligations. There are moments, however, when we need to cut ourselves a break.

Here's a silly example. Let's say you have an unreasonable fear of rhubarb. You get near a rhubarb pie, and you feel your chest tighten. You get lightheaded. You're a true rhubarbaphobic. You know, as a person trying to nurture your own spirit, that you have to confront your fears, but today you're really tired. It's okay to say, "Those tart stalks have hounded me for years now, and I'm going to engage in a little avoidance behavior today. I'm not going into that kitchen because, I'm sorry, I've got rhubarbaphobia."

Occasionally, when you don't have the strength, you can acknowledge what you're doing, take the easy way out, and still respect yourself in the morning—occasionally.

☺☺

Striving to better, oft we mar what's well.
WILLIAM SHAKESPEARE

Echo question:
Have you found some silence yet?

Toward the beginning of this book I asked if you could spare fifteen minutes per day to sit quietly and relax, and I want to revisit that question now. It's becoming crucial that you find a daily time of silence. Stop and think for a moment. You're reading this modest book, asking yourself questions, finding some answers, coming up with new and beautiful questions of your own, listening for the wisdom of those around you, and hopefully (and most importantly) growing in your awareness of the Divine presence in your life. With all that is going on, you need time to work in your body, mind, and spirit. If nothing happens in the stillness, that's okay; imperceptible healing is going on. Sometimes, however, as you sit quietly, your spirit learns things your mouth can't say. A path that once seemed obstructed is cleared, and you can't say why. Suffering that sits in your chest blossoms into a delicate blessing you never expected. And, to be honest, you enter into full and necessary sadness. In short, what the spirit needs it gets in silence.

@@

Habit, my friend, is practice long pursued,
That at last becomes the man himself.
EVENUS

Echo question:
Are you still fighting for control?

If the truth be told, I'd like to ask 732 questions in this book, and 366 of them would be this one. I'd like to ask it every day, but that would get pretty boring after a while. I do think, however, that control is the central issue of spiritual peace.

When you try to control your life and the lives of those around you, your spirit is like a sparrow with a Cadillac attached to its leg. It can't fly.

I would like to suggest that you install in yourself a control meter that you look at frequently. When you feel despair, check to see if you're trying to fly with a "luxury" car tied to your leg.

⊚⊚

In his prayer he says, thy will be done:
but means his own, at least acts so.
WILLIAM PENN

Are you always certain?

People of great faith sometimes make a very serious and self-defeating mistake: they don't allow for doubt in their beliefs. The problem with certainty is that it often requires denial, and denial creates tension. How much more faithful it is to place even our beliefs and convictions in God's hands, to confess that we're not sure about all things, even the little things; to confess that underneath our masks all of us are a bit confused and afraid. Don't worry about hurting God's feelings and incurring God's wrath. God's ego is big enough to accommodate our faithful doubt.

@&

I believe; help my unbelief!
MARK 9:24

Is *spirituality* a *private matter?*

Time to get tough: tending our spirit is *not* like weeding a garden behind our house that no one knows about. I think it's self-deception to suppose we can hear an inner call to peace without also seeing that the world is in tears. The problem is, most mainstream Christian denominations have quietly condoned, and their leaders embraced, the notion that our religion is nobody's business but our own.

Sitting blissfully in our living rooms and churches and never walking out our doors is pretty much the same as knowing our neighbor's house is burning down and not calling the fire department. Our world is on fire and you can't sit still and watch. You are called to be God to those who are suffering. Time to get moving.

◎◎

> *Genuine faith is not only concerned with*
> *privately being a "good person," it is also concerned*
> *with making the world a better place*
> *in which to live through public action.*
> BRENNAN R. HILL,
> PAUL KNITTER,
> AND WILLIAM MADGES

Do you understand
the limitations of philosophies?

Once we gain comfort and direction from a new way of thinking, we want to keep thinking that way. We like having a dependable method of dealing with life; however, sometimes we get so swallowed up by our philosophical outlook that we can't see truth staring us in the face. For example, in Voltaire's famous literary work *Candide,* the character Pangloss believes that everything happens for the best. The work, a satire on optimism, contains numerous scenes of unbelievable violence and cruelty, many of which end with Pangloss explaining how each event contributed to the best possible ending. Pangloss can never see the limitations of his philosophy, but we should have the brains and courage to see beyond ours.

❀

The philosophies of one age have become the absurdities of the next, and the foolishness of yesterday has become the wisdom of tomorrow.
SIR WILLIAM OSLER

Where is your home?

That I used the word *where* in this question is telling. We think of home as a place, or we might say that home is wherever our family is. Unfortunately, reality with a jagged edge threatens these two concepts of home; places burn and people die.

Over the past few years, I have come to change my definition of home from a "where" to a "who." When I sit still and open myself to God's presence, then I'm at "home." This doesn't detract from the comfort I find in my house or the love I feel for my family; rather, my home in God's presence affirms the reality that I'm never homeless, even if I'm alone and without shelter.

◎◎

Where Thou art—that—is Home.
EMILY DICKINSON

Are you afraid to die?

Everyone's at least a little bit afraid of death, and those who claim otherwise are probably lying. Acknowledging fear and wondering about our afterlives are healthy activities for the soul, certainly preferable to stifling our natural apprehension about death only to be greatly disappointed when our bell tolls and we discover that we are not as brave as we had thought. We need to allow ourselves to feel what we feel about death and not pretend. Only in this way can we cultivate within ourselves a faith in God's goodness and move peacefully through the eternal dance.

᭳᭳

The fact is, we cannot truly face life
until we have learned to face the fact
that it will be taken away from us.
BILLY GRAHAM

Are you living simply for the afterlife?

For centuries the Christian mind-set has held that this world is crummy and evil and that we ought to reject the earthly and embrace the world to come. I find this sensibility unacceptable. Although people sometimes make the earth a lousy place, the earth itself is beautiful and we ought to enjoy it while we are here. After all, we don't know if we'll even have senses in the hereafter, so we should take in all the sights and sounds and smells we can. The other reason I have trouble with the "wait for the next world" mentality is that many of the people who think this way make "the next world" a ridiculous place where only those who adhere to a strict but arbitrary moral code get in. I can't accept this extreme either. I simply refuse to believe that we were created to be consigned to oblivion after a handful of years. I believe the next world will be great, but we ought to enjoy this one while we're here.

@@

Earth's crammed with heaven,
And every common bush afire with God.
ELIZABETH BARRETT BROWNING

What would you do if today were your last day to live?

You may have heard this question before, but it's worth bringing up again. People who have had near-death experiences report that their lives have since become more simple for them, that they can see their priorities more clearly. Perhaps we all should try to live today as if we might not have a tomorrow on this earth.

☺☺

Nobody has ever died wishing that they'd spent more time at the office.
UNKNOWN

Where is God?

I heard a wonderful meditation recently on the Divine in humanity: When man and woman were created, they rejected their divinity. The counsel of angels then tried to decide what to do with this gift that man and woman had given up. One angel suggested that they bury divinity within the earth; another suggested they hide it at the bottom of the sea; yet another said they should place divinity up in the stars. After discussion, the angels concluded that humanity would gain the ability to reach all these places and find their divinity.

Then one angel said, "Let us hide divinity deep within man and woman themselves. They'll never think to look there." And so they did, and today we travel the centuries-old peace path, forgetting time and again that we're not walking toward God, but with God.

@@

Canst thou by searching find out God.
BOOK OF JOB

Echo question:
Still hoping for your circumstances to change?

Hope for change is a formidable and persistent obstacle to peace. I realize that it's hard to resist "dreaming of a better tomorrow," but unless our situation is intolerable (e.g., people are treating one another or themselves badly), we need to recognize and celebrate what's at hand. I imagine that if you're reading this book, a house plant, a tree, a cup of tea, the smooth face of a child, a breeze, laughter in the distance, or a slow walk are at your disposal. Although we have to allow ourselves to be human, to occasionally sigh at the beauty of a dream, we also have to pray that God will open in us space for joy in what surrounds us.

வ௫

The sparrow is sorry for the peacock
at the burden of its tail.
RABINDRANATH TAGORE

Can loss be a gift?

A friend of mine is a recovering alcoholic. Although he's been sober for almost ten years now, he still bears the scars of his disease. He lost a wife and a job. At least he thought of this as loss at first; however, the marriage was a destructive burden for both of them. What's more, he was terribly unhappy with his job, which had something to do with his drinking in the first place.

Over the years, my friend has come to view his loss as a gift. He's not happy about the pain he and his ex-wife went through, but he realizes that losing that marriage and job made room for better experiences in his life—like a healthy relationship with another woman, an engaging life as a college student, and a rich spirituality.

What he perceived as loss was, he later learned, a clearing out of his life, painful in the way a woman must lose what's inside of her to receive a baby.

✿

You must lose a fly to catch a trout.
GEORGE HERBERT

Do you honor periods of discernment?

Although we are in a hurry to get possessions we're sure we need, we're even more impatient when it comes to making major decisions. We want to be settled mentally, to have our lives lined up for the next ten years, and we feel threatened by changes in the plan. Unfortunately, we fail to recognize, appreciate, and respect those periods when we just don't know where we're headed and what the future will hold. When we struggle against our uncertainties, we flail about, setting our minds on one course only to be derailed in the very next moment. It's far more peaceful to admit that we're in a process of discernment. We need to love ourselves enough to slow down and to think.

☙❧

Be not swept off your feet by the vividness
of the impression, but say, "Impression, wait for me
a little. Let me see what you are and what you
represent. Let me try you."
EPICTETUS

Do you give others space for discernment?

When we love people, our happiness depends in some measure upon their well-being. I realize that this can become codependency if taken too far; nevertheless it's reality for most of us. We don't need to deny that we want our loved ones to be happy, but we should not let our own peace be entirely compromised by the struggles, pain, and discernment of others. If we rush a loved one or if we try to take over her or his decisions, we're not doing our job. We must stand by, support, listen, and understand.

◎◎

Truth resides in every human heart,
and one has to search for it there
and to be guided by truth as one sees it.
But no one has a right to coerce others
to act according to his own view.
MAHATMA GANDHI

Do you play the wise elder?

The more I think about the wise people I have known in my life, the more I'm struck by how little advice they offer me; moreover, I can't remember a single instance of them "pulling rank" on me by claiming to be older and, therefore, wiser. As a result of their restraint, I come to them often for guidance.

If I were to list their names here, they would be uncomfortable, for they're self-reflective, painfully aware of how much they don't know. They don't *play* wise elders; they *are* wise elders.

❧

How prone to doubt, how cautious are the wise.
HOMER

*Do you sometimes go further
than you should in seeking answers?*

Questions, sometimes irrelevant and small ones, burn in our heads and hearts, and we want answers so badly that we overlook the cost of extracting them. In various situations in my own life I have pestered and pressured loved ones for information, and at least a few times the pain I caused was far greater than the relief I experienced in "knowing." When folks are ready to talk, then they'll talk. To force them to do so causes injury and only replaces one kind of suffering with another. Best to let go of the need to know.

☯☯

*He that breaks a thing to find out what it is
has left the path of wisdom.*
J. R. R. TOLKIEN

Do you live with integrity?

I love the word *integrity*. I think it's one of the richest words in the English language, for it connotes honesty, compassion, dignity, and intellect. Integrity also suggests that we enable others to live with integrity. Integrity is letting the cashier know he charged you too low a price for the dish soap. It's listening to the panhandler's rambling. It's assuming the guy in the wheelchair is just like you are. It's taking the time to think through a troubled friend's options when there don't appear to be any options left.

Professional, personal, spiritual, intellectual integrity—I don't think you can stay on the peace road without it.

◎◎

Integrity can be neither lost nor concealed nor faked nor quenched nor artificially come by nor outlived, nor, I believe, in the long run denied.
EUDORA WELTY

Echo question:
Are you still wondering why things happen?

Although I must confess I never get caught up in this question, I'm aware that lots of other people do. As I listen to them mull over the cause-effect relationships they see in the world, one theme comes through: the grand design. When bad things happen, especially to good people, one question is inevitable: Why is the grand design dumping on me? For this reason, I think comforting ourselves with the notion of a grand design is ultimately unhealthy. Best to open our minds and spirits to what is, to live fully in what is, to accept and deal with what is.

꩜

Knowledge is proud that he has learn'd so much;
Wisdom is humble that he knows no more.
WILLIAM COWPER

Can two opposing views both be right?

One of the reasons that multiculturalism has met with much resistance in our society is that we tend to think in terms of "one way or the other, but not both." The motto of many is, "There can be only one winner." Actually, the world is a lot more gray than it is black or white. The more comfortable we are with gray, the more we can see the validity of conflicting views and the more we enable ourselves to be at peace. Of course, this peace comes with a price: sometimes there aren't clear answers to life's large and small questions, and we might appear weak to others if we say so. But, then, appearing weak doesn't create a problem for a peaceful person.

෨෧

Be not righteous overmuch.
ECCLESIASTES 7:16

Can you welcome cultures
different from your own?

The peaceful spirit is generous, roomy, tolerant. There is simply no excuse for turning up our noses at people who cook differently, behave differently, believe differently. Remember, each person you meet is as much God's child as you are.

ꙮ

Learn never to conceive a prejudice against others, because you know nothing of them. It is bad reasoning, and makes enemies of half the world.
WILLIAM HAZLITT

Can you deal peacefully
with cultures you find objectionable?

After we've given those different from us a chance, we might feel like getting mean. For example, the Western world finds the oppression of women in various Eastern cultures repulsive. If we would like to help women who are oppressed, how should we do so? The more we struggle and threaten, the more oppressors dig in their heels; if change is possible, I bet we'd get further with love and understanding. In any case, violence does no good and love can do no harm.

☮☮

Be of them that are persecuted,
not of them that persecute.
THE TALMUD

Do you know your religion's history?

If you are a member of a specific denomination, it's important to do some reading on its history. Doing so provides a larger context within which you can view present teaching. We tend to think of religious doctrine and tradition as fixed, yet a glance at nearly any church's history shows frequent change. For example, most Lutheran church bodies did not ordain women as pastors until about twenty-five years ago. Also, until the second Vatican Council of the 1960s, Roman Catholic doctrine said that salvation was reserved for Catholics alone.

Acknowledging changes like these reminds us of timeless truths and helps us gain perspective on doctrinal issues that can make us uncomfortable in our own worship communities.

◎◎

It is in the uncompromisingness with which
dogma is held and not in the dogma
or want of dogma that the danger lies.
SAMUEL BUTLER

Is there room at your table
for one more person?

The peaceful spirit is open, welcoming. If you often feel as though you'd rather not have certain people around, then you are more concerned about orchestrating situations than about being loving and showing compassion in every situation. Besides, if you're excluding people, then you're probably tense when you don't have control over who is in your presence and who is not. To cultivate peace within yourself, always make room at your table for one more person.

@⊚

Grasp the whole world of reason, life and sense,
In one close system of benevolence.
ALEXANDER POPE

What did you (or will you) eat today?

When we think about spirituality, we often forget that God is also incarnate in each of us physically and that we need to nurture that aspect of our spiritual selves. We don't need to be nutrition fanatics, but we should eat wisely and moderately most of the time. When we're careless about what we put in our bodies, we neglect a piece of the Divine.

On a more practical level, when we eat wisely we have more physical and intellectual stamina. Although I've made much the same suggestion elsewhere in this book, I'd like to recommend that you develop a habit of consciously choosing what foods you eat and noticing how they make you feel. Just as important, pause before you eat to reflect on the gift that sits before you.

∽∽

The belly is ungrateful—it always forgets
we already gave it something.
RUSSIAN PROVERB

Echo question:
Are you a fun person yet?

I want to revisit this question because at times peace seeking takes on the form of work. Perhaps you read one of these questions each day and have fit some quiet time into your daily routine. As with any discipline, however, what begins as fresh and exciting marches on toward grinding obligation. Remember, the peace journey ought to be seasoned with laughter and spontaneity.

☺☺

We torment ourselves rather to make it appear
that we are happy than to become so.
LA ROCHEFOUCAULD

Do you like to see people punished
for their crimes?

When people argue in favor of stiff prison sentences or capital punishment, they often claim that stiff penalties will deter others from committing crimes. I suspect that what such people are trying to do is validate their own desire for revenge. If you are gratified to see people punished, reexamine your position. Taking pleasure in punishment, no matter how seemingly just, is merely anger and hatred manifesting themselves. Let go of revenge.

@@

No punishment has ever possessed enough power
of deterrence to prevent the commission of crimes.
On the contrary, whatever the punishment,
once a specific crime has appeared for the first time,
its reappearance is more likely than its
initial emergence could have been.
HANNAH ARENDT

Whom do you trust?

A few weeks ago I was in a class in which the teacher asked the students to make a list of people or things they had faith in. Since I was sitting in on the class, I decided to make a list too. Mine was short: (1) The will of God; and (2) the spirit of the Divine as it lives in people of conscience.

Don't misunderstand me. There are people in my life whom I trust, but I also realize that we all fail, that we often unwittingly resist the Divine that lives in us. As you can see, I include myself in this "us."

What impact does this realization have for our trusting in individuals? Perhaps it makes our trust more compassionate and forgiving. If we understand that most people want to be trustworthy and that their failure seldom constitutes personal betrayal, we will be quicker to bounce back when those we love disappoint us.

@@

Trust in God, but tie your camel.
PERSIAN PROVERB

Is formal punishment necessary?

Let's face it: some people need to be locked up because they're a danger to society; others need to be detained until they can be rehabilitated. So is detainment necessary? Absolutely! But is punishment necessary? I don't think so. In fact, it is yet another form of violence. If we jail people with the goal of seeing that they either do not have the chance to commit crimes again or are reformed, then we are not punishing. Our need to punish those who commit crimes fills prisons and expresses societal anger, but that's about it. In the end, criminals punish themselves through their own acts.

☉

Revenge is a kind of wild justice,
which the more man's nature runs to,
the more ought law to weed it out.
FRANCIS BACON

Do you hold yourself above the criminal?

I don't pretend to know how God sees things, but if the parent-child metaphor captures our relationship with God, then even the most vile criminal we see hauled off to prison on the television news is beloved. I believe that God loves us all equally and that some folks' lives go wrong for reasons we can't begin to understand.

Our temptation is to feel proud of ourselves when we see others' weaknesses, but when we strive to see with love's eyes, we know God's love for all who suffer and cause suffering. We share God's suffering. And we realize our weakness, our proximity to those we're tempted to call monsters.

֍

Should you see another person openly doing evil, or carrying out a wicked purpose, do not on that account consider yourself better than him, for you cannot tell how long you will remain in a state of grace. We are all frail; consider none more frail than yourself.
THOMAS À KEMPIS

Are you nosy?

If you think about it, being nosy is a lot like being hungry. Once you hear a bit of gossip, it's like eating one potato chip or one bite of chocolate—a little isn't enough. You can't stop until you're stuffed. If you accept this comparison, then perhaps you'll also agree that the hungers for gossip and junk food spring from the same source: that place in our spirits we're all trying to fill and can't. Maybe we should think of being nosy as yet another reflection of our longing for God that we keep trying to fill in a foolish, unhealthy way.

@@

When you are told a rumour do not swallow it
like a hungry pike. Say "Show me your facts."
And before you accept them be sure they are
the whole facts and not half facts.
UNKNOWN

Can you keep a secret?

If being nosy is like hungering for junk food, then telling secrets is like baking a chocolate cake and eating the whole thing with a friend. More than this, you've used a stolen cake mix. There is plenty of room for secrets in the quiet soul.

@@

Tell no tales about friend or foe;
unless silence makes you an accomplice,
never betray a man's secret.
BEN SIRA

Do you tweak the truth?

We all know that truth is a slippery thing; in fact, in most situations, we're probably better off speaking of "truths" than of a single "truth." This being said, if the truths we can discern get tweaked and nibbled on enough, then only falsehoods remain. For example, the other day I was talking with an old friend about a teacher I once studied under in college. My friend said, "There was a story going around about her. Her classes were pure chaos, and nobody learned a thing. Her students all agreed to give her great evaluations because she gave everyone an 'A.' Is that true?"

"Not true at all," I told him.

Over time, the truth had been pinched and embellished enough that actual harm has been done. Perhaps some small falsehoods are harmless—but I have my doubts.

@@

If you add to the truth,
you subtract from it.
THE TALMUD

Do you believe in prophecies?

As a teacher of college writing, I read at least a couple of student papers per year about the end of the world. Students look at Scripture or the writings of a mystic or two and argue that our demise is just around the corner. I try to look sympathetically on the fallacies and lack of historical awareness that inevitably pepper such compositions, but inside I always say to myself, "What's the difference?"

The more time I spend in prayer and contemplation, and the more I speak with peaceful people, the less I worry about knowing ahead of time what's going to happen to our world and how. Trying to dissect prophecies is just another way of trying to gain a measure of control over life—can't be done. I think it's better to spend our energy on figuring out ways to heal God's face of hunger, illness, oppression, and despair as we see it revealed in millions of our brothers and sisters the world over.

◎◎

I always avoid prophesying beforehand,
because it is a much better policy
to prophesy after the event has already taken place.
SIR WINSTON CHURCHILL

Echo question:
Do you love having your ideas challenged?

One instinct we have when people ask us to defend our opinions is to take the challenge personally. We figure that if folks are looking for faults in our views, then they are really looking for faults in us.

When we get past feeling assaulted, we move on to use the challenge as an opportunity to articulate our ideas and grow from the wisdom of others. The peaceful person isn't afraid of hearing new and even threatening ideas; rather, he or she is confident, knowing that all ideas should in some manner serve light and life, healing and nurturing.

@@

If you would convince others,
seem open to conviction yourself.
LORD CHESTERFIELD

Do you argue fairly?

I recently read an article in a men's magazine that let me know how to win an argument. Like many other writers on this subject, the author concluded that you don't need to have reason on your side to win. You just have to know the right persuasive strategies.

The peaceful person doesn't care about winning arguments, but about finding the truth, even when it appears to come at her or his expense. Someone who just wins an empty argument goes home to a cold house. Someone who has learned a truth is warmed on the way home.

☙❧

Positive, adj. Mistaken at the top of one's voice.
AMBROSE BIERCE

Do you have endurance?

Endurance is having the peace within to pursue suffering if it is productive or necessary. A friend of mine is a good example of endurance. For almost a year now, his dad has been in a nursing home after suffering kidney failure and a stroke. He is not in his right mind. Every time my friend visits his dad, and this is almost every day, his dad says, "I want to go home. You never come to see me. Don't bother coming anymore. I hate you." Day after day my friend shows up to visit his dad. My friend realizes that his dad isn't thinking clearly, and so his love overcomes his dad's senility. My friend has endurance.

◎◎

Two frogs were playing on the rafters of a dairy barn one night. They fell into adjacent pails of cream. They jumped and hopped and scrambled for survival. One fought the good fight longer and harder than the other, and stayed the course. When the farmer came in the next morning, he found one frog floating on the top of a pail of cream, dead, and the other standing on a cake of butter, exhausted but happy to be alive.

FATHER GILES BELLO

Do you get derailed
by the impatience of others?

As you grow toward peace, patience, and endurance, you will notice yourself being tested all the time. The impatience of those around you is magnetic. You respect people's needs and want to hurry to please them; however, you must honor your own pace in this life. Doing things at a pace comfortable for you is really the only way you can do things well, so to hurry for people is to do them no favor.

∞

Nothing great is created suddenly,
any more than a bunch of grapes or a fig.
If you tell me that you desire a fig,
I answer you that there must be time.
Let it first blossom, then bear fruit, then ripen.
EPICTETUS

Echo question:
Have you turned off
that radio and television yet?

I made an interesting discovery over the past six months. Sometimes being in silence is hard work. I say this because I've been guilty of overworking myself during this time, and I found that it was much easier to sit quietly and read or just be still when I wasn't working twelve hours per day. The noise of a sitcom or a song that moves distracted me from fatigue and unhappiness.

Perhaps many of us share this same struggle. The conclusion I've come to is that room for God's whispering presence is more important than extra money. I've taken some steps to solve the problem. How are you doing?

@⁄@

> *Elected Silence, sing to me*
> *And beat upon my whorlèd ear,*
> *Pipe me to pastures still and be*
> *The music that I care to hear.*

GERARD MANLFY HOPKINS

*Do you keep going to doctors
in search of wellness?*

I have no medical training, but over the years I've watched loved ones spend thousands of dollars on doctors who prescribe one drug after another and achieve little success. I've often felt sure that the source of suffering brought to doctors is spiritual. The medical community is learning more each day about the effects of stress and the power of the human mind, and it is beyond debate that psychological pain can bring about physical suffering. If you are taking lots of medication and going to doctors and aren't feeling any better, you might also speak to a psychologist. Maybe your soul is suffering through your body.

෨෨

*There is a wisdom in this beyond the rules of physic.
A man's own observation, what he finds good of
and what he finds hurt of, is the best physic
to preserve health.*
FRANCIS BACON

Is there vanity in your peace?

An inevitable part of the peace journey is closely watching the lives of others, not as voyeurs but as curious observers. We are called to share what we know in hopes of presenting the face of God to those we meet each day; however, we need to be aware of our motives. If we reach out to people, we should do so because we believe in the possibility of our helping, not because we want others to see us as wise or powerful. Vanity with noble purposes is still vanity. When trying to offer assistance, our prayer should be, "God, let me be an effective instrument of your love."

✺✺

It is in vain that we get upon stilts, for, once on them,
it is still with our legs that we must walk.
And on the highest throne in the world
we are still sitting on our own ass.
MICHEL DE MONTAIGNE

Do you bring contemplation
to your community?

I've discovered over the years that if I don't take time
to quiet my heart and open my spirit to the Divine, I
have nothing to bring to the communities in which I
live and work. Worse, when I fail to let love and compassion (the fruits of healthy solitude) guide my actions, I can actually do harm to those around me.

The woundedness of society seems to call us to
be swift and violent. To get on in this world, we are
told, we have to step occasionally on the backs of
others. When we sit still and clear our minds, however, we brush such messages from us like dried mud
from our jeans and hear deep in ourselves the spiritual realities that we can bring to our communities:
kindness, patience, generosity, forgiveness, reconciliation, cooperation.

@@

*When you have shut your doors and darkened your
room, remember, never to say that you are alone;
for you are not alone, but God is within,
and your genius is within.*
EPICTETUS

Are you always early?

Good friends respect each other's time, but sometimes we forget to respect our own time. We're so concerned with punctuality that we get physically knotted up over being five minutes late for commitments. If this is true for you, try not to be so hard on yourself. It's easy to rob yourself of an hour's worth of peace over two red lights and a train you weren't planning on; moreover, if you get bugged by being late, chances are you like things to be just so and get in a bad state over trivialities. When faced with maddening details, focus on breathing and relaxing. Don't waste yourself on small matters.

@/@

Life is eating us up. We shall be fables presently.
Keep cool: it will be all one a hundred years hence.
RALPH WALDO EMERSON

Are you a perfectionist?

The person who is strict about punctuality is often a perfectionist, which can be a self-destructive tendency. If you don't believe this, just ask perfectionists. One of the biggest troubles they face is overcoming their fear of failure and trying new things. The result, especially for college students I've advised, is procrastination. For example, a student puts off doing a research paper because she thinks she's a poor writer. Finally, two days before the paper is due, she does a twelve-hour stint at the library, spends one sleepless night scanning the material, and frantically writes the paper on the last night. What happens? Her fears are confirmed. She gets a lousy grade. And so the snake continues to bite its own tail. If all of this sounds familiar to you, explore your desire for perfection. Valuing flaws as a part of life's process is one way to loosen up.

∽∾

Do not seek to have everything that happens happen as you wish, but wish for everything to happen as it actually does happen, and your life will be serene.
EPICTETUS

Do you feel guilty
when you miss your quiet time?

I know a lot of people who have developed the practice of observing a daily quiet time. Some practice contemplative prayer or Zen meditation; others read; still others just sort of hang out. As we discuss our experiences, one common theme emerges: nobody's perfect. It's common for people to miss a day or two now and then. Folks who lead busy lives might even fall asleep during their quiet time.

The point of establishing a practice of silence is to make a rich life of the spirit part of the ebb and flow of our days. We shouldn't get obsessive and turn a beautiful practice into a source of anal-retentive guilt.

ᕲᕲ

To go beyond is as wrong as to fall short.
CONFUCIUS

Do you have any bad addictions?

Thus far in this book I've asked you in various ways to consider your appetites and how they reflect a vague hunger that can only be filled by the Divine. Most of us possess such appetites, but they are downright deadly for some of us. Today, at this very moment, search yourself and admit to yourself any dangerous addictions. If you have an addiction that may shorten your life (e.g., addictions to work, alcohol, tobacco, drugs, serious overeating), let this be the day you remember as the beginning of your healing. Let this be the day you begin opening your heart to God in hopes of satisfying your soul.

ॐ

*Mr. Lely, I desire you would use all your skill
to paint my picture truly like me, and not flatter
me at all; but remark all these roughnesses, pimples,
warts, and everything as you see me,
otherwise I will never pay a farthing for it.*

OLIVER CROMWELL,
TO PETER LELY,
WHO WAS ABOUT TO PAINT HIS PORTRAIT

Do you cultivate healthy passions?

On the whole, it's probably best for people seeking spiritual peace to live lives of moderation; however, within the context of a balanced life, there's room for healthy passions. In the late autumn each year, for example, my wife and I have a passion for drives through the acres of vineyards that line the shore of Lake Erie in Pennsylvania. We roll down the windows, feel the cold air rush in, and smell the grapes. It's like we're driving through a sea of grape juice.

What are your healthy passions? Chess? Reading? Picnics? Find, celebrate, and cultivate your healthy passions.

☯

Set out wisely at first; custom will make every virtue more easy and pleasant to you than any vice can be.
ENGLISH PROVERB

Are you willing to get help?

There are some problems we simply can't solve on our own; however, seeking help from a therapist or even from a friend might make us feel weak. The truth is, we are never stronger than when we look realistically at ourselves, see that we are in over our heads, and tell our problem to somebody who is trained to help. We simply can't dance when we are shackled by suffering and are not in the process of healing.

☙❧

Discover someone to help shoulder your misfortunes.
Then you will never be alone . . .
neither fate, nor the crowd,
so readily attacks two.
BALTASAR GRACIAN

Are you trying to escape?

Many people know Sophocles' story of Oedipus the King, but here's a reminder. When Oedipus was young, he learned of a prophesy that he would kill his father and marry his own mother. "So," thought Oedipus, "I'll move far away so this will never happen." He does so, unaware that those he thinks are his parents are really just guardians. On that road, Oedipus kills his father and eventually marries his mother. In the end he gouges out his eyes.

How's that for a cheery story? The point is, even though our own destinies are not so loathsome as Oedipus', our efforts to escape the inevitable just lead us to it. So the question is, how do we escape the maelstrom? My answer is, dive in headfirst. Generally speaking, our destiny isn't the problem; we are. If something is really destined to happen to us, the only thing we have some control over is our reaction to destiny. If we know that God is with us and in us, fate's jagged edges are polished smooth.

@@

The efforts which we make to escape from our destiny only serve to lead us to it.
RALPH WALDO EMERSON

Echo question:
What is wealth?

You already know the answer to this, but it is time to move it again into the front of your mind. I do so because I know from my own peace journey that it takes a long time to part with happiness buying. In fact, I should make a confession. Since I started writing this book, I've made a number of happiness purchases. True, I could claim to need the stuff I bought, but in my own mind I know I was out there trying to purchase a little piece of God. I'm not trying to be a joyless heavy here, but when we slap another $500 or $1,000 on our credit card at 18 percent, we should at least be aware of what we're up to.

◎◎

Riches rather enlarge than satisfy appetites.
THOMAS FULLER

Echo question:
Do you respect yourself yet?

In the course of writing this book, I have spoken to lots of people about spiritual peace. One characteristic I see in lots of people seeking spiritual peace is low self-esteem. I agree that humility is becoming, but at some point it crosses over into self-loathing.

Actually, there's a lot to respect in all of us. God's dwelling within us makes each of us worthy of esteem. Maybe this sounds trite, but I mean it. Some people say they believe that God is always present within and about them; then they "invite" God to be their guest. If God is in us, then we can all claim esteem, not because of what we do, but whose we are.

✺

It is difficult to make a man miserable
while he feels worthy of himself and
claims kindred to the great God who made him.
ABRAHAM LINCOLN

Are you willing to suggest that others get help?

If getting help ourselves seems threatening, telling somebody else to get help is even worse. Yet it appears that the more serious a person's problem, the more unlikely he or she is to acknowledge it. "You need to get counseling" can be a friendship-ending statement, but not speaking out can be a life-ending sin of omission. A person at peace can't remain silent while a loved one deteriorates.

@

*There is always a way to be honest
without being brutal.*
ARTHUR DOBRIN

Do people have a biological predisposition to certain behaviors?

Since I am a college teacher, I can be permitted one trick question in this book. I believe that a peaceful person wouldn't concern herself or himself with why people behave the way they do. Although we should always try to understand those we love, we should not judge. The question above speaks of judgment, not of unconditional love.

@@

Let love be genuine;
hate what is evil, hold fast to what is good;
love one another with mutual affection. . . .

ROMANS 12:9

Do you love animals?

If the philosophy of Christian stewardship of the earth has one unfortunate result, it is that human beings see themselves as the most important beings on the planet. However, if we are more important than animals, why is this so? Because we are animals who talk, that's all. Being at peace means loving and seeing as equals those who cannot speak for themselves.

⊚⊘

anthropocentric: 1. that considers man as the central fact, or final aim, of the universe. 2. conceiving of everything in the universe in terms of human values.
WEBSTER'S NEW WORLD DICTIONARY

354

Are people fundamentally good or bad?

For many years, centuries in fact, Christians have mourned the innate depravity of humanity, which holds that we are inherently dirty, yucky, lustful, sinful beasts unworthy of God's love. This view of ourselves makes us feel like finding a good cliff to jump off rather than dancing; fortunately, there is another way to look at ourselves: We are God's creation, inherently good but marred by human weakness and imperfection. To be at peace we need to accept our fundamental goodness and trust that God will help us to fully realize it.

☺☺

I am simply a human being, more or less.
SAUL BELLOW

Echo question:
Are you spotting the sacred gifts yet?

As I write this, I am sitting in the presence of more gifts than I can count. I'm working at a picnic table on a beach, and each leaf in the trees around me is trembling in a hearty wind. Lake Erie goes from pale brown, to pale turquoise, to something like aquamarine, then to the horizon. The people scattered around me are enjoying one another, the sun, the water. Kids are getting sand in every crevice of their little bods, and, yes, men and women are checking each other out.

A lecturer I heard recently said, "Once you start seeing the gifts around you, it gets ridiculous really. There's no way of counting them all." Make it part of your spiritual practice to see and give thanks for the blessings crowded atop the cosmic dance floor.

◎◎

Some men never find prosperity,
For all their voyaging,
While others find it with no voyaging.
EURIPIDES

Can you pick up your cross
and show it to others?

There is great power in community. Just knowing that we are not alone in our struggles keeps us going sometimes. For example, when people who are battling addictions discover that scores of others are engaged in the same fight, the war somehow seems winnable.

As a person on the peace journey, you have a wonderful opportunity. Sharing your cross with others is a gift. Let them look at it, run their hands across it, ask questions about it. Then watch something magical happen. Slowly, this cross turns into an intersection where wounded souls converge, where burdens are lifted, where healing glistens like streetlights in a misty rain.

✪✪

People are crying up the rich and variegated plumage
of the peacock, and he is himself blushing
at the sight of his ugly feet.
SA'DI

Can you play like a child?

There is a freedom in childhood that we seem to spend our entire adult lives trying to recapture. The key to doing so is to reject self-consciousness. When kids are playing, they could care less if they have chocolate smudged on their faces or if their underwear is hanging out of their pants. All they care about is the pleasure and intensity of the moment. Can you lose yourself in play? Can you take a walk in the rain? Can you let ice cream drip on your Bermudas? Are you as wise as a child?

@/@

Age does not make us childish, as they say.
It only finds us true children still.
JOHANN WOLFGANG VON GOETHE

Do you ask "why" the way a child asks "why"?

If you really want to learn the true nature of things, ask "why" the way a child does. If we keep asking enough times, we find out the real motives of our actions. For example, let's say you have a five-year-old daughter who wants to stay up late on a Saturday night. You want her to go to bed at her usual bedtime of 8:30 P.M. "Why do I have to do to bed?" she asks.

"Because little girls need lots of sleep," you say.

"But why can't I stay up? I can just sleep in."

"Because if you stay up this Saturday night, you'll want to stay up every Saturday night."

"Why can't I do that?"

If this daughter asks why enough, you'll hit a wall—and the truth is right behind it. Although she should go to bed and get lots of good sleep, you want her to go to bed mostly so that you can relax. Try this self-questioning in just about any situation, and you'll find some enlightening answers.

๑๑

Life is an unanswered question, but let's still believe in the dignity and importance of the question.
TENNESSEE WILLIAMS

Echo question:
Is the time you're taking
for your peace journey important?

If you've been talking to people about your peace journey, or if you even mention the word *spirituality*, you may get blank stares that mask scorn. Despite the booming sales of self-help and inspirational books, few people pay attention to their spiritual needs and, as the Salinger quote below says, people who do are thought of as weird.

Don't let that stop you. I believe that the time you take to commune with the Divine is the centerpiece of your life; it's a thread running through your day. Think of it this way: it takes only five minutes a week to fill the gas tank of your car, but you could go nowhere without spending that five minutes. The presence of God runs the spirit as gasoline does a car.

◎◎

. . . it's very hard to meditate and live a spiritual life in America. People think you're a freak if you try to.
J. D. SALINGER

Echo question:
Figured out what'll make you happy yet?

Millions of people the world over need their situations to change before they can be happy. It's tough to be happy when you go to bed hungry, when you're afraid to go out at night because folks get killed in your neighborhood, when your husband might beat you tonight or he might not.

But let's also face something else: not all, but most of the people reading this book already have all they'll ever need to be happy. This is not to say that you are not at this moment going through a struggle; rather, I'm offering two reminders: (1) Most of the time, we have no idea what will make us happy and are disappointed when we get what we asked for; and (2) it's easy to get into a funk waiting for things to make us happy.

There are many valid reasons to be unhappy. If you don't have one, a day of gifts is awaiting you.

◎◎

Our wills and fates do so contrary run
That our devices still are overthrown;
Our thoughts are ours, their ends none of our own.
WILLIAM SHAKESPEARE

Do you watch carefully for the truth?

When I teach literature courses, I tell my students that there are limitless "right" ways of interpreting texts and that as long as they can defend their interpretations, no problem. I add quickly, however, that there are wrong interpretations. Those "wrongs," I tell them, crop up when they embrace what fits their reading and conveniently ignore what does not.

To illustrate this point, I ask students to examine one of the most misinterpreted poems in American literature, "The Road Not Taken" by Robert Frost. When we read the poem carefully, we can see that Frost's speaker admits that both of the roads he stands before are the same, so when he says at the poem's end that his taking the road less traveled by "has made all the difference," he is, in fact, kidding himself. I write this not to trash people's affection for the poem, but to encourage a commitment to truth and a determination not to overlook wrenches that get thrown into our smooth-running machines.

☺☺

Read, not to contradict and confute;
not to believe and take for granted;
not to find talk and discourse;
but to weigh and consider.
FRANCIS BACON

Does trouble touch your core?

Perhaps the greatest treasure of our earthly cosmic dance is that with prayer and meditation comes the development of a center that remains largely untouched by much of the nonsense of daily life. The snarl of a co-worker, the sour gallon of milk we just brought home from the store, the broken keepsake on our mantle don't seem to disrupt our days as much as they used to. We don't get shaken by small tremors anymore.

Are you feeling this peaceful, God-filled center growing within you? It's too much to claim that big troubles don't rock us, that even puny garbage doesn't clog us up once in a while, but what a treasure it is not to feel fragile in the face of every encounter, not to feel like a fresh wound exposed to the air of all jagged words. We can claim God incarnate in our human center and walk with courage through fields of broken glass.

⚚

All fortune belongs to him who has a contented mind.
Is not the whole earth covered with leather for him
whose feet are encased in shoes.
PANCHATANTRA

Can you claim the promise?

For a number of years now I have been giving stress management workshops, and the longer I do them the more difficult they become for me. Most of what I deal with are symptoms, but in a workshop designed for general consumption, I don't generally speak at length about the ultimate stress reducer—a fundamental trust that our Creator is good and loving, that our purpose for being here on earth is not to suffer, that we are not meant to spend our time shaking with anxiety, that our Creator's will for us is not to be damned.

Most "wisdom literature" I've read reinforces this point. In some traditions the promise of divine grace is clearly and forcefully articulated; in others it is implied. Regardless of our religious orientation, one of the most powerful actions we can take to "manage" our stress is to claim the promise of the Creator's love for us.

@@

To work hard,
to live hard, to die hard,
and then go to hell after all
would be too damned hard.
CARL SANDBURG

What do you want from this journey?

It's ironic: the more time we sit still in silence, the more we see the ceaseless motion of our spirits. Sometimes we're sprinting, other times wandering or dancing in circles. What drives us crazy about this movement is we don't know the destination. Sure, we have a basic idea about where we'd like to be spiritually; for example, we'd like to feel ever-increasing amounts of contentment. But we don't know where we're going to end up or what will be best for our spirits.

The hardest part about faith is handing *everything* over to God, even the journey. As we walk down a path that requires us to let go of our wishes, we hold tight to the notion that at least we'll be at peace. Now here's the kicker: we've got to let go even of the notion we'll be at peace. I know it sounds paradoxical, but it's true. Being at peace necessitates that, for the love of God, we'd be willing to give up peace. And that's when peace comes.

☙☙

Faith is to believe what you do not yet see;
the reward for the faith is to see what you believe.
SAINT AUGUSTINE

Do you believe in the cosmic dance?

If you have reached these last couple of pages, I'm going to permit myself the hope that the questions herein have been a companion to you as you walk an endless path toward and through peace.

Before we end this conversation called a "book," however, I would like to return to the starting point and formally ask the implied question of the title: Do you believe in the cosmic dance? In other words, do you think we do things to ourselves and one another that keep us from the central joy of humanity—the cosmic dance? Are you trying to be there, to walk, wander, stumble with others on the way to and through that place of dancing?

ºº

. . . no despair of ours can alter the reality of things, or stain the joy of the cosmic dance which is always there. Indeed, we are in the midst of it, and it is in the midst of us, for it beats in our very blood, whether we want it to or not.

Yet the fact remains that we are invited to forget ourselves on purpose, cast our awful solemnity to the winds and join in the general dance.

THOMAS MERTON

What are your questions?

As this book closes, I hope you have discovered that it raises more questions than it answers. That's as it should be. For every mystery we unravel, many new mysteries are born. "After every *no*," the poet Wallace Stevens writes, "there comes *a yes,* and on that yes the future world depends." Each time we seem to hit a finality, a *no*, something beautiful beyond calls out, something that holds a new truth. I pray you keep asking questions that lead you to the never-ending cosmic dance, where the only things we can be sure of are that there are more questions than answers, that we are loved just as we are, that we must love others as they are, and that, as God has promised, we are never alone.

๑๑

Young Rabi . . . went to the public schools
and stood at the top of his class with little effort.
He remembers vividly how
his mother would tirelessly inquire,
"Did you ask any good questions in school today?"
FRANCES BELLOW

Bibliography

Bartlett, John, ed. *Bartlett's Familiar Quotations*. Boston: Little Brown, 1980.

Dale, Edgar, ed. *The Educator's Quotebook*. Bloomington, Ind.: Phi Delta Kappa Educational Foundation, 1984.

Ehrlich, Eugene, and Marshall De Bruhl, eds. *The International Thesaurus of Quotations*. New York: Harper-Perennial, 1996.

Gleason, Norma, ed. *Proverbs from Around the World*. New York: Citadel Press, 1995.

Gross, John, ed. *The Oxford Book of Aphorisms*. Oxford: Oxford University Press, 1988.

The Oxford Dictionary of Quotations. Oxford: Oxford University Press, 1970.

Safire, William, and Leonard Safire, eds. *Words of Wisdom*. New York: Simon and Schuster, 1989.

Seldes, George, ed. *The Great Thoughts*. New York: Ballantine, 1985.

Index

About the Author

John Coleman is a professor of writing and literature at Mercyhurst College, as well as a published poet and essayist. He lives in Erie, Pennsylvania, with his family Kathy, Elena, and Micah.